Successful Educational Leadership in New Zealand

Case studies of schools and an early childhood centre

Edited by
Ross Notman

NZCER PRESS
Wellington 2011

NZCER Press
New Zealand Council for Educational Research
PO Box 3237
Wellington 6140

© Ross Notman 2011

ISBN 978-1-927151-37-2

All rights reserved

Designed by Cluster Creative

Printed by Prestige Print, Wellington

This title is also available as an e-book from www.nzcer.org.nz/nzcerpress

Distributed by NZCER
PO Box 3237
Wellington
New Zealand
www.nzcer.org.nz

Contents

Foreword		5
Acknowledgements		7
Chapter 1	Leading New Zealand Schools and Centres: An Introduction *Ross Notman*	9
Chapter 2	Learning-centred Leadership: A Case Study (Peter Verstappen, Southbridge School) *Susan Lovett*	15
Chapter 3	Leadership Located and Locatable (Georgina Kingi, St Joseph's Māori Girls' College) *Hine Waitere*	27
Chapter 4	Philosophical Leadership: Mike's Story (Mike Sutton, Rototuna Primary School) *Jeremy Kedian*	39
Chapter 5	Relational Leadership in a Primary School Setting (Richard Newton, St Clair School) *Darrell Latham*	51
Chapter 6	Leadership Focused on an Ethic of Care (Richard Inder, Gate Pa School) *Alaster Gibson*	63
Chapter 7	Collaborative Leadership in a Specialist School (Jann Carvell, Fairhaven School) *Lynn Tozer*	75
Chapter 8	A Holistic Approach to Leading a School (Larry Ching, Waimea College) *Annie Henry*	87
Chapter 9	Whānau Leadership in Early Childhood (Hinerangi Korewha, and Aroaro Tamati, Te Kōpae Piripono) *Kate Thornton*	99
Chapter 10	Cultural Change and Moral Leadership (Mark Brown, Victory School) *Paul Potaka*	111
Chapter 11	Invitational Leadership: A School where Students Inhabit the Digital Space (Colin Dale, Murrays Bay Intermediate) *Colin Dale and Richard Smith*	123
Chapter 12	Building Leadership Success in a New Zealand Education Context *Ross Notman*	135
Editor and contributors		153

Foreword

Being invited to write a book's foreword is a privilege—probably the result of one's advanced years! However, in responding to Dr Ross Notman's request, feelings of being somewhat humble but touched come readily to mind. The concept of leadership in educational (and other) contexts has filled many hours of my wakeful thoughts. For me, leadership is the most powerful of concepts. Yes, in learning places, many aspects are important—planning and strategy, assessment and evaluation, appraisal and performance, management of staff and resources, development of curriculum, to name a few. But the overarching concept is that of leadership which, in simple terms, might be described as "the exercise of influence." It is leaders who make things happen, who motivate and excite, who must be "out front" in seeking improvement, who foster and articulate the prevailing culture that embody where "our" place is going and how it seeks to get there.

The ten case studies of educational leadership in this edited collection fulfil a number of purposes. First, they illustrate the work of experienced and successful leaders as people and professionals, noted as being "exemplary practitioners." Each case is carefully analysed by someone of rich experience and deep thought about leadership and education. My good fortune has been to be associated with most of these writers. Their chapters not only are based on solid data but also each discussion draws on the wider literature. Underpinning the entire research project were the methodological guidelines of the International Successful School Principalship Project, undertaken in 14 countries, setting the book within a context extending well beyond our shores.

These case studies are characterised by their contemporary, real-world nature clearly reflected in the emphasis of each chapter: invitational leadership, cultural change and moral leadership; shared, holistic, collaborative and caring leadership; professional learning; leadership that embodies respect and integrity plus learner-centred leadership. Each approach speaks to us today! The other strength of the chapters lies in the reflective questions that are posed for readers and the suggested further reading.

This is a realistic book. It does not simplify the principalship. It does not tell people how to do the job. It does not present recipes for instant success. This is much more of a thinking person's book about a small group of New Zealand educational leaders. Each one is presented as a real person doing a real job in today's world—the challenges, the approaches, the successes, the people themselves. While telling their story, each contributor presents their interpretation of a specific leadership context.

Most importantly the reader is well positioned to make his or her own judgements, comparisons or translations of situations, underpinning beliefs and actions that are encountered in their reading. For me, this is a very real strength of this book in that it will encourage educational leaders to reflect on their own values, goals and practices against the various case studies in the book. Would I have done the same thing? Why did the principal act in that way? How would I have handled that situation? What can I learn from this case to improve my own performance? Ross, himself, helps us in this process in the final chapter with his discussion of central concepts like pedagogical leadership, contextually responsive and connected leadership, as well as the self-awareness that underpins inner leadership. The outcome of such a book must be more effective leadership in educational places!

This book is a timely resource for principals and early childhood leaders, those who aspire to leadership positions, academic researchers and teachers about leadership in education, in addition to those who plan, implement and sponsor professional development programmes. I congratulate Dr Ross Notman and each of his contributing team of researchers for their work in substantially moving forward our thinking about educational leadership.

Emeritus Professor Wayne L Edwards, OBE
Massey University
and
President
International Pacific College
Palmerston North, New Zealand

August 2011

Acknowledgements

I would like to acknowledge with gratitude the contribution of the following individuals and organisations.

Emeritus Professor Wayne Edwards graciously agreed to write the foreword. Wayne is a longstanding member of the New Zealand educational leadership community and was the instigator of educational administration programmes of study while at Massey University.

Phil Davison gave permission to publish extracts from his leadership poem, based on reflections of Canadian tertiary leaders.

The University of Otago Research Fund provided financial support, which made the research study and editing process possible.

The National Council of the New Zealand Educational Administration and Leadership Society gave strategic support for the book's publication in line with its aim to strengthen cross-sector understanding of educational leadership in New Zealand.

Finally, I would like to record my appreciation to the 11 contributors who engaged with the respondents, analysed data and reported their findings on successful leadership. As a research team we sincerely thank the educational leaders for their time and experiences that have been so willingly shared with others.

Ross Notman

CHAPTER 1

Leading New Zealand Schools and Centres: An Introduction

Ross Notman

The dissonance and grace of leadership

A 24/7 public possession
running as fast as I can
with hooks in me.

Need a 20-year-old body
and 60-year-old mind
to avoid the cross-eyed vortex of minutiae
stay awake to the imaginative
and resist the flow.

(Davison & Burge, 2010, p. 111)

As part of a Canadian study of educational leaders' experiences at tertiary level, Phil Davison penned the opening stanzas of a poem using words from respondent interviews to reflect the complexities and pressures of leadership. You may well recognise parallels between the poem's theme and the demanding realities of leadership across all education sectors and across positional leadership roles including principals, deputy and assistant principals as well as teacher leaders. Despite the challenges of leading in contentious times, inspirational stories abound of how school principals and early childhood centre leaders have contributed to the learning of society.

This book features case studies of 11 New Zealand educational leaders, both as testimony to the extraordinary work of these leaders and to help aspiring, new and experienced practitioners understand more about their leadership role. The book will reveal some of the exhilaration of being a leader in different school/centre settings. It will also identify the key values, attributes and strategies that have enabled them to achieve and maintain success. However, for the benefit of readers unfamiliar with educational developments in New Zealand, a brief overview will be given of the national context of educational leadership. This will be followed by an exploration of the origins of the book through its link to the International Successful School Principalship Project (hereafter referred to as ISSPP).

Context of New Zealand educational leadership

Compared with centralised education systems in some countries, the New Zealand educational leadership context is different in its decentralisation of governance and its emphasis on self-managing schools. Beginning in 1989, the management of New Zealand primary, intermediate and secondary schools was devolved from a central government agency to boards of trustees elected by local parents. Each board is expected to exercise its governance function on a multitude of educational issues, such as systemic educational reform, school effectiveness, assessment, school operations and school-based management. This includes legislative, judicial and executive roles such as the appointment of staff.

The expectations of a New Zealand principal therefore changed dramatically after 1989. Challenges for principals in this self-managing environment arise from both outside and inside the school. In a section entitled "The *real* world of the secondary school principal", part of an Education Review Office (1997) report on the professional leadership of secondary principals, the impact of the external social setting was made very clear. Principals' descriptions of this environment were particularly pessimistic at the time:

> They saw family violence, sexual abuse, absence of discipline in the home, lack of parenting skills, low educational expectations and students who were out of control, a loss of traditional values, lack of respect for authority, disruptive students, truancy, vandalism, lack of support from outside agencies, drug and alcohol abuse, and racial tensions as insurmountable pressures on their working lives. (Education Review Office, 1997, p. 31)

Hodgen and Wylie (2005) claim that earlier reforms in educational administration, fundamental changes to the New Zealand school curriculum in 1993, a new qualifications framework, and the role of the Education Review Office compounded the principal's workload. In addition, the introduction of professional standards for principals and teachers, and national standards for years 1–8 primary children helped raise public expectations of schooling within a market forces model of education.

However, acknowledgement of the changing circumstances and expectations of educational leaders has resulted in a number of support mechanisms for principals, in particular the development of a conceptual model of Kiwi Leadership for Principals (Ministry of Education, 2008). At the centre of this framework is educational leadership where school leaders work across four interconnected areas of practice—culture, pedagogy, systems, and partnerships and networks—all of which are bounded by relationships. Leading change and problem solving are seen as key activities for leaders. The model also identifies four essential leadership qualities: manaakitanga (leading with moral purpose), pono (having self-belief), ako (being a learner) and āwhinatanga (guiding and supporting). Elements of the model find expression in a range of national professional development programmes offered to aspiring, new and experienced principals. For example, the National Aspiring Principals' Programme focuses on four areas of leadership practice: culturally responsive leadership, leading change, leading learning and developing self.

In addition to the context of primary and secondary school leadership, it has been noticeable in the New Zealand non-compulsory education sector that the needs of early childhood leaders are gaining momentum in the leadership literature (Fasoli, Scrivens, and Woodrow, 2007; Thornton, Wansbrough, Clarkin-Phillips, Aitken, and Tamiti, 2009). In an occasional paper published by the New Zealand Teachers Council, Thornton et al. advocate for a national leadership policy for early childhood education, and for models of leadership that include features such as distributed leadership approaches, mentoring, opportunities for reflection, and ongoing leadership development programmes. It is apparent that educational leadership is now being accorded the recognition it deserves as a pivotal influence in the purposeful learning environment of children of all ages. Such recognition is justified by the findings of the ISSPP research project.

ISSPP findings and methodology

Under the auspices of Professor Christopher Day at the University of Nottingham, the ISSPP began in 2002. The now 14-country (including New Zealand) research project aims to move research attention away from effective schools to focus on factors behind principals' success (Jacobson and Day, 2007). The findings from an initial group of countries (England, the USA, Australia and Norway) identified successful principal practices in instructional leadership, capacity building and organisational learning, and cultural diversity (Ylimaki, 2007).

The ISSPP was replicated in New Zealand using the research questions and protocols employed in the international studies. These questions focus broadly on similarities and differences across national educational contexts, the impact of accountability measures and different socioeconomic backgrounds, and particular leadership strategies and characteristics that contribute to a successful principalship. In view of the New Zealand self-managing school environment and the need for principals to forge strong connections with their board of trustees and wider community, a supplementary question of interest was: "To what extent is a successful principalship in the New Zealand context contingent upon a successful relationship between a school and its community?"

Multi-site case study methods were employed for this phase of the New Zealand research study in 2010 using a total sample of 10 cases—one specialist school, one early childhood centre, one intermediate school, five primary schools and two secondary schools— to reflect the principle of "maximum variation sampling" (Maykut and Morehouse, 1994). The size of the institutions range from an early childhood centre of approximately 25–30 children, to a secondary school with a projected roll of 1,500 students. There are seven male and four female leaders in this study, covering a spread of geographical locations throughout the North and South Islands of New Zealand.

Case study leaders were selected against two ISSPP criteria: (1) the school/centre had received a positive external and independent inspection report by the Education Review Office, particularly with regard to the leadership and management of the leader; and (2) the principal/leader was widely acknowledged by their professional peers as being effective and successful in their role. Guidelines from the ISSPP methodology informed the development of a schedule for two educational leader interviews, observational protocols, and the use of inductive cross-case analysis (Miles and Huberman, 1994). On these bases, 10 case studies of successful New Zealand educational leaders were developed.

Structure of the book

The cases chosen for this book highlight the dispersion of educational leaders' accomplishments throughout New Zealand, the variation in leadership styles and strategies that bring about and sustain leadership success, and the different contexts in which children's learning takes place. The cases are reported in a variety of ways: some studies link emerging leadership themes to a research base, while others present the case in the form of a narrative or dialogue that allows readers to theorise their own data. The title of each chapter represents a dominant style that is characteristic of the educational leader and a starting point for readers' subsequent reflection.

In Chapter 2 Susan Lovett describes a learner-centred principalship in a rural town in Canterbury. This primary school principal demonstrates the importance of a strong connectivity between school and community, in which the principal leads through personal strengths of modelling best practice and liaising with parents.

In Chapter 3 Hine Waitere traces the experiences of a female leader of a Māori Girls' College in the Hawke's Bay region. This example of situational leadership shows the power of contextual awareness on the part of the principal within a Māori cultural and educational environment.

Jeremy Kedian explores the leadership of a Hamilton primary principal in Chapter 4. In this case, leadership success is founded upon personal professional learning that has influenced the principal's understanding of social capital and trusting relationships, and their particular impact on organisational effectiveness.

Building on this theme of relational leadership, Darrell Latham presents a study of a Dunedin primary principal in Chapter 5. This urban school leader sees respect, integrity, a personal regard for others, and his own professional competence as important factors behind his success.

In Chapter 6 Alaster Gibson reports on a case of leadership that is focused on an ethic of care. This Tauranga principal has a strongly values-based form of leadership, which has helped transform a failing primary school into a caring and innovative learning community.

In Chapter 7 Lynn Tozer illustrates the story of a successful principal of a specialist school in Napier. It is an account of collaborative leadership by a woman who builds the professional capacity of her teachers and promotes a family culture within the school.

A holistic approach to leading a Nelson co-educational secondary school is the theme of the case study outlined by Annie Henry in Chapter 8. Here, the principal regards holistic development as being just as important to himself as it is to his students and staff. His own resilience is a precursor to supporting resilience in others.

In Chapter 9 Kate Thornton writes about a shared leadership role in a Māori immersion early childhood centre in New Plymouth. The centre illustrates the concept of whānau (family) leadership, whereby the two lead teachers encourage a community in which everyone can lead, and parents', students' and teachers' contributions are all valued.

A Nelson primary principalship is portrayed by Paul Potaka in Chapter 10 as an example of cultural change and moral leadership. In this school the principal is driven by a vision of educational and social justice that seeks to sustain learning success for a multi-ethnic student population and for their parents.

In Chapter 11 Colin Dale and Richard Smith jointly depict a successful intermediate school principalship in Auckland in terms of invitational leadership. Here the objective is to motivate, through dynamic and innovative programmes, students and staff to participate in a technology-focused process of teaching and learning.

In the final chapter Ross Notman synthesises the case study findings about successful educational leaders in New Zealand under four topic headings: pedagogical leadership, professional leadership, interpersonal leadership and intrapersonal leadership. This discussion chapter argues for a re-conceptualisation of the role of educational leader given the impetus for democratic forms of decision making and leader accountability.

Each case study chapter in this book concludes with a series of diverse reflections for the reader, together with suggestions for further reading. The editor and writers hope that these reflective comments and questions will encourage aspiring and current educational leaders to think critically about their own workplace practices. We hope, also, that readers will draw inspiration from this sample of successful New Zealand principals and early childhood leaders who have dedicated their professional lives to making a difference for students.

References

Davison, P., & Burge, E. J. (2010). Between dissonance and grace: The experience of post-secondary leaders. *International Journal of Lifelong Education, 29*(1), 111–131.

Education Review Office. (1997). *The professional leadership of secondary school principals.* National Education Evaluation Reports, No. 4. Wellington: Author.

Fasoli, L., Scrivens, C., & Woodrow, C. (2007). Challenges for leadership in Aotearoa/ New Zealand and Australian early childhood contexts. In L. Keesing-Styles & H. Hedges (Eds.), *Theorising early childhood practice: Emerging dialogues* (pp. 231–253). Castle Hill, NSW: Pademelon Press.

Hodgen, E. & Wylie, C. (2005). *Stress and well-being among New Zealand principals.* Wellington: New Zealand Council for Educational Research.

Jacobson, S. L., & Day, C. (2007). The International Successful School Principal Project (ISSPP): An overview of the project, the case studies and their contexts. *International Studies in Educational Administration, 35*(3), 3–10.

Maykut, P., & Morehouse, R. (1994). *Beginning qualitative research: A philosophic and practical guide.* London, UK: Falmer Press.

Miles, M. B., & Huberman, A. M. (1994). *Qualitative data analysis: An expanded sourcebook.* Thousand Oaks, CA: Sage.

Ministry of Education. (2008). *Kiwi leadership for principals.* Wellington: Author.

Thornton, K., Wansbrough, D., Clarkin-Phillips, J., Aitken, H., & Tamiti, A. (2009). *Conceptualising leadership in early childhood education in Aotearoa New Zealand.* Wellington: New Zealand Teachers Council.

Ylimaki, R. M. (2007). Introduction to the special issue: International Successful School Principal Project (ISSPP). *International Studies in Educational Administration, 35*(3), 1–2.

CHAPTER 2

Learning-centred Leadership: A Case Study

Susan Lovett

Peter Verstappen
Principal, Lismore Primary School (1997–1998)
Deputy Principal, Ashburton Borough School (1999–2006)
Principal, Southbridge School (2007–present)

Introduction

This case study illustrates one school principal's attempt to connect leadership with learning. Peter Verstappen's ways of drawing in staff, students and community to create and implement a vision for his school's curriculum can be framed in terms of *learning-centred leadership* (Southworth, 2009). This type of leadership distinguishes school leaders from leaders of other organisations in that it signals a "desire and responsibility to enhance students' learning" (Southworth, 2009, p. 91).

Southworth suggests that principals "explicitly seek and want to make a difference to the schools they lead" (p. 92). A case study of a principal striving to be such a leader is of interest because it offers an entry point for exploring principals' conceptions of leadership and the ways in which leadership intentions can be enacted within particular contexts to influence student learning and achievement. The data underpinning this case study were drawn from multiple sources, including interviews, observations and document analysis, as part of a larger longitudinal project (2007–2010) called 2020VISION (Lovett, Verstappen, Clarke, and Gilmore, 2010). When analysing this material we adopted Simons's (2009) preference for "situated generalisation," because this approach enables the reader to "discern which aspects of the case they can generalize to their own context and which they cannot" (p. 165).

Background: The principal and the school setting

Peter Verstappen was a late entrant to teaching, having previously worked as a professional actor, broadcaster and, for 10 years, producer of a children's television show. He has worked in three schools in the roles of teaching principal, deputy principal of a large primary school and, for the past three and a half years, principal of nine teachers at Southbridge School, an hour's drive from Christchurch (New Zealand).

Southbridge is a small rural town with a strong core of middle-class families who have lived in the district for multiple generations. New Zealand schools each have a designated decile rating, which is an indicator of socioeconomic status. Southbridge School has a decile 9 rating, the second highest on this scale, along with a higher percentage of Māori students than is typical for a rural Canterbury school. Owing to the growing demand for dairy workers and the fact that Southbridge is within commuting distance of Christchurch, new families have begun to move into the district. Cheaper housing means the area is affordable to beneficiaries. In addition, new arrivals from other countries have added a second-language dimension to the school. Overall, the children are well prepared for school and keen to learn, while their parents appear to value education and what the school has to offer. Parental engagement is a particular strength of the school and gained a special mention in the 2009 Education Review Office evaluation report.

He uses reciprocal dialogue at every opportunity, through both direct conversations and the written word

Peter connects with teaching and learning in the school through a range of strategies for monitoring teacher and student performance. These include "learning-walks" through classrooms, where he looks for evidence or artefacts of learning on display and talks to the teachers and children about their work. He uses reciprocal dialogue at every opportunity, through both direct conversations and the written word.

Peter's enthusiasm for learning permeates his every action and serves to reinforce the purpose of schooling. He wants, and expects, responses to his questions about learning and demonstrates his interest in the satisfaction to be gained by students in new learning experiences. At times he even quizzes the children at the school road-crossing about their day at school. Students willingly share examples of their learning when they meet Peter in the classroom and about the school. They are left in no doubt that he is keenly interested in their learning, not only because he continually asks them about their experiences but also because he works with them to create new and exciting learning opportunities. One example is Peter's endorsement of an idea from two of the senior boys who were keen for the new playground area to include a skateboard ramp. These boys were delighted to find not only that their suggestion became a reality but also that they were invited to draw plans for its design. Peter's responsiveness to their suggestion increased their sense of belonging, and in turn helped the boys' engagement with learning. They now had a good reason for coming to school!

The New Zealand curriculum revision: An opportunity

Peter welcomed the requirement in the new (2007) New Zealand curriculum document that every New Zealand primary school should design and implement its own local curriculum. After realising that the new-entrant cohort of 2007 would finish their formal schooling (Year 13) in 2020, he devised the name 2020VISION for this project. He also invited researchers from the University of Canterbury to collaborate in the initiative and to act as mentors. By enlisting the support of academics with whom he had worked previously (before taking on the principalship at Southbridge), Peter was able to add another layer to the data used to develop the school curriculum to ensure the curriculum reflects the unique needs and aspirations of the local community.

Although the research project accompanying the development of 2020VISION was a novel idea, it gave the project added status in the school and the community, especially as the university team was often at the school and made a point of being visible and approachable to the students, parents and teachers. As a longitudinal study, the project has tracked the evolving nature of the school's curriculum and the leadership actions underpinning its development. In particular, it has tracked the ways in which the consultation process has drawn in teachers, parents and students as collaborative learning partners in contributing ideas and commitment to an evolving 2020VISION.

Newsletters invite dialogue about learning

All schools are required to consult with their communities, but Southbridge goes much further than most by actively encouraging and inviting parents to engage in ongoing dialogue about learning. A variety of approaches are used to include parents in activities, such as parent focus groups, 2020VISION days, and sports, cultural and academic events. One key strategy is the school's newsletter, which is distributed weekly by email or in hard copy to parents and community members. Although the newsletters serve an educational function in sharing news of daily life at the school, families are also invited to respond to questions and to share their experiences in regard to the children's learning and activities. Peter takes pains to ensure all parents find this approach invitational rather than simply informational. This notion of invitational leadership practice signals to parents that their voices matter in shaping the school as a learning community.

Peter carefully crafts his introductory remarks in each newsletter to engage and entice readers. The language he uses is accessible, and he frequently includes storytelling to capture moments of learning. The tone of the newsletters conveys a genuine interest in gaining a response, and the parents do, in fact, take the time to reply verbally or by email to Peter as principal. In addition to inviting comment, the newsletters often contain questions or topics for families to discuss at home. Peter also encourages students to share their suggestions or questions with him, and he makes sure he is always a highly visible and interested presence around the school.

This notion of invitational leadership practice signals to parents that their voices matter in shaping the school as a learning community

School–community partnerships

Peter views the school–community partnership as an integrated whole and uses the symbol of a triangle to encapsulate the equal roles the home, the school and the pupil play in children's education. The triangle, with points connected by lines, draws attention to the relationships each of the three partners has with the others. In a newsletter to parents (30 April 2009), Peter explained the nature of this partnership:

> When it is working well, this triangle is incredibly strong and gives the child the best possible start in life. But if any single element of the triangle is weakened, it disables two-thirds of the structure and the triangle collapses. The dreams and ambitions we have for our children's education will only happen if we make this triangle work.

Peter's main aim is for students to see their lives at school and beyond school as one. His aim is for students and parents to see that education is not like "forcing the membrane at nine a.m. to enter the school and forcing oneself out at three p.m. to resume normal life." Rather, he promotes the notion of a "vanishing school", by which he means "school, home and community will cease to be mutually exclusive learning environments in the minds of children." In a similar vein, Peter also talks about inside-out and outside-in learning, of which the school's Trees for Learning project is a prime example. Southbridge has begun to develop gardens containing native plants at the school and on nearby Rakaia Island, in partnership with the Ministry for the Environment and a local nursery. Peter explained this development, and what the school hoped from it, in a newsletter sent out to parents and community members on 29 May 2008.

> These native gardens will become an important part of our 2020VISION curriculum. We intend to improve and extend them over the years ahead, to involve all our children in their development and to use them as a base for environmental education projects. Years from now we want our children to return to the island and to school and admire their trees. Is this what you mean?
>
> Our native gardens are also a response to our discussions about how we want learning to be at our school as we move towards 2020VISION. We've heard from the community (and we believe this ourselves from our knowledge of good teaching and learning) that you want your children to experience "real" learning that has purpose beyond exercise books and worksheets. We also hear that you think it is important that learning connects with the community. You may have already volunteered to help our planting day at the island next Friday. If not, you are welcome to join us. And we want your feedback.
>
> Is this the kind of learning experience you think is valuable?
>
> Is this what you mean?
>
> Let me know, Peter.

The learning dialogue at Southbridge School provides an entry point for formulating and progressing the 2020VISION. The implicit challenge is to change the way everyone associated with the school perceives schooling. Under this vision, the school is seen not as a transmitter of knowledge but as an organisation directed towards helping children develop learning habits that will serve them for a lifetime.

For us, this thinking has helped explain the relevance and importance of our research. The case study approach has allowed us to explore three important questions concerning children's learning:

- To what extent do parent and teacher relationships with children promote or inhibit their education?
- To what extent do home–school relationships foster student learning?
- In what ways does the school's community enable its children to learn?

Discussions about learning

We found another example of how the school's newsletter serves as a catalyst for discussions about student learning in one issue advertising a family maths evening (14 August 2009). Peter began the newsletter with three maths problems and offered two free tickets to a rugby game to the first person to reply with the correct answers. In the next paragraph he reminded parents of the ways in which people apply mathematical skills in daily life. Following this, he provided examples of all aspects of maths (measurement, geometry and number).

> Whether or not maths is your 'thing' it still figures enormously in your life, and in the life of your child. By the time you read this newsletter on Thursday afternoon, you will have used maths a dozen times today, from something as simple as knowing when to set your alarm ... to judging the distance between the front of your car and the curbing when you park outside the school.

Peter then went on to describe the forthcoming maths week and invited parents to attend a family maths evening. The evening, he wrote, would include shared activities and workshops on how to support children's maths learning at home.

Throughout the research project we witnessed many other invitations to parents to support school learning on the home front. We saw ready recognition among school staff, parents and other interested community members that the questions Peter asked tended to be difficult and would require a fundamental shift in perception about learning. We were also aware that not all members of the school's community could, or would, respond to every invitation, and that reaching these people required an approach that was both creative and persistent. The newsletter, with its real examples of learning and active illustrations of how learning matters, was one way of keeping parents and students aware of the focus of 2020VISION.

Successful leadership strategies

Peter considers his most important work in the school to be building stronger school–community partnerships. However, he is also quick to point out that such "success is only as good as the last encounter with parents. What worked yesterday may not work today or tomorrow." He is particularly mindful that successful school leadership does not reside solely with the principal, no matter how enthusiastic, dedicated and energetic he or she may be. He wants to build leadership capacity and distribute leadership at the school, but he knows that this can only happen if the school has a highly experienced staff.

For Peter, extending leadership beyond the staff with formal designated roles has not been easy. He explains that the annual turnover of staff (most moving to larger schools) and their replacement with beginning teachers has slowed the pace of the 2020VISION project. The absence of more experienced teachers has made it difficult for him to distribute responsibilities in the school. However, this situation has improved with the appointment of a new deputy principal, whom Peter sees as bringing considerable strengths in home–community partnerships, the Māori community and literacy. A new senior management role in the school, involving an assistant principal and a rōpū[1] structure, has also been instituted.

He is also quick to point out that such "success is only as good as the last encounter with parents. What worked yesterday may not work today or tomorrow"

Peter also works hard to create spaces for parents who have the time, energy and inclination to contribute to enhancing learning at the school. For example, Southbridge School now provides opportunities for parents to be members of parent focus groups, and for senior students to take on roles on student learning committees covering a range of interests, such as the environment, sports and the arts. Students are also encouraged to make presentations about their learning and to join in discussions during 2020VISION development days.

Leading through personal strengths

The school–community partnership approach Peter has taken in developing the 2020VISION project marks him as a learning-centred leader. The manner in which 2020VISION has reinforced the importance of learning and the way this emphasis has been nurtured and sustained ultimately come down to Peter's personality as a performer. Southworth (2009) claims that

> effective leaders know they are 'on show' ... Not only are leaders closely observed, but what they pay attention to gets noticed ... Leaders who visit classrooms, encourage colleagues to talk about their teaching successes and concerns, and ensure that meetings of teachers focus on learning, demonstrate that they remain strongly connected to classrooms. (p. 96)

---

1 The school is divided into the two rōpū of the teachers of Years 1–3 and of Years 4–6. Each is led by a member of the senior management team. The rōpū is another name for a grouping of teachers working with similar-aged children.

Peter acknowledges the link between performing and his role as school principal. He freely admits to playing roles with intent rather than by default, and acknowledges that his strengths in performance contribute to his resilience in the face of the daily challenges of being a principal. He attributes his ability to "put on and off a professional costume, demeanour and role with a degree of ease" to his years in theatre. Although Peter is the force behind 2020VISION, his energy, persistence and creative responses have also gathered the support and commitment of the school and the community.

In Peter, the research team sees a leader who knows that connecting leadership with learning is about working with and developing people, being open to ideas, and adjusting the pace of change and development to suit the understanding and energy of others. However, Peter's success also comes from distributing leadership, for, as he emphasises in word and practice, leadership must extend beyond the principal as a person.

As a leader Peter is sustained by ideas and the networks of people around him. His mantra, a principle he not only states but also models to staff, is "keep looking up, out and accept challenges." He believes there are two choices for a principal: to help *make* opportunities happen, and if this is not possible, to go out and *find* opportunities. These choices characterise Peter as a learning-centred leader, as someone who actively seeks to combine leadership with learning and to have this principle explicitly practised by everyone associated with Southbridge School. That leadership should be linked with learning is also a dominant theme in *School Leadership and Student Outcomes: Identifying What Works and Why* (Robinson, Hohepa, and Lloyd, 2009), with its key message that "the closer educational leaders get to the core business of teaching and learning, the more likely they are to have a positive impact on students" (p. 47).

Keep looking up, out and accept challenges

The role of school leadership in student achievement and well-being

The claim that leadership makes a difference to student achievement and well-being was confirmed through our study and its review of associated literature. The aforementioned work of Robinson et al. (2009), with its eight dimensions relating to the qualities and effects of school leadership,[2] offers a framework for identifying

---

2 The eight dimensions are: (1) establishing goals and expectations; (2) resourcing strategically; (3) planning, coordinating and evaluating teaching and the curriculum; (4) promoting and participating in teacher learning and development; (5) ensuring an orderly and supportive environment; (6) creating educationally powerful connections; (7) engaging in constructive problem talk; and (8) selecting, developing and using smart tools (Robinson, Hohepa, and Lloyd, 2009).

leadership for learning. Notably, the synthesis revealed that school leaders who take an active role in educational development have significant direct and indirect influences on children's learning, and the same applies to the case study principal described in this chapter.

Southworth (2009) endorses the connection between leadership and learning, stating that leadership is "more potent when it focuses on developing students' learning and strengthening teaching" (p. 93). He also maintains that when learning-centred leaders add their influence to that of the teacher, it can create a combined effect on students' learning. However, because leadership contexts vary, and thus necessitate different actions, there is no formula for successful leadership for all situations (Leithwood, Jantzi, and Steinbach, 1999). In this respect, case studies of leadership are useful because they allow us to recognise the uniqueness of different contexts and, in doing so, collectively expand our knowledge of leadership actions and their effects.

Southworth (2009) further emphasises the difference between leadership and the leader. By viewing leadership as an activity or a set of actions, it becomes possible to move beyond the idea of the formal position of leadership and to recognise the many actual leaders in schools who may not necessarily hold official leadership roles. Harris and Muijs (2005) contend that "distributed leadership enables expertise to be recognised wherever it exists rather than seeking this only through a formal position or role" (p. 28). Peter Verstappen acknowledges this in welcoming and forging opportunities for others to share leadership responsibilities at Southbridge School, regardless of whether they are teachers, parents or students. This is also why Robinson, Hohepa and Lloyd (2009) take particular care in their research review to include all types of leaders and leadership roles rather than focusing solely on principals.

> *It becomes possible to move beyond the idea of the formal position of leadership and to recognise the many actual leaders in schools who may not necessarily hold official leadership roles*

The 2008 OECD report *Improving School Leadership* is another document that redefines school leadership responsibilities for improved student learning as the responsibility of a wider group of leaders. This is further endorsement of the need for learning-centred leaders who can use their leadership actions to support the learning and achievement of others, which is exactly what Peter is doing at Southbridge School. The OECD report redefines these responsibilities in terms of what leaders can do to:

- support, evaluate and develop teacher quality
- support goal-setting, assessment and accountability

- enhance strategic financial management skills of school leadership teams
- adopt a systematic approach to leadership policy and practice. (p. 64)

Each of these actions requires what Bush (2009) refers to as knowledge for understanding, for action and for improvement of practice, and for the development of a reflexive mode. These same areas of knowledge are all hallmarks of a learning-centred leader like Peter: a principal who is constantly making deliberate connections to further his own learning and that of others.

One strategy for valuing these connections is to create and review educational visions. Southworth (2009) refers to this very point in terms of "a sense of direction" in relation to the explicit purpose of schooling. This means having a vision and the plans to translate the vision into action:

> Leaders look ahead to see what is on the horizon and what this means for the school. They are aware of those patterns and trends outside the school which will have implications for the students' learning needs today and tomorrow. They then work towards developing the people and the organization to meet the challenges and seize the opportunities the perceived changes may have for the students, the staff and the school as a whole. (Southworth, 2009, p. 94)

Conclusion

The influence that Peter Verstappen exerts as a principal, and the way he exerts it, appears to be closely aligned with the three strategies that Southworth (2009) outlines in his learner-centred leadership framework of modelling, monitoring and dialoguing. Peter places learning at the forefront of his work, whether it be his own learning as a leader or his leadership actions to promote learning among students and the parent community. As a leader, his focus on learning is deliberate and always present in conversations about the key purpose of schools.

The importance of fostering learning relationships and connections with the parent community is also endorsed by Robinson et al. (2009), who name and devote a whole chapter to this theme in their best evidence synthesis iteration. They advocate the "ako" (learning and teaching) principle in order to signify the fundamental importance of reciprocal learning and teaching for the creation of educationally powerful connections between home and school. Part of this means that principals must also be learners who demonstrate a willingness to learn from and listen to others' voices if they are to bring the worlds of home and school together to improve students' learning. Such a focus on alignment is achieved through leaders "utilising opportunities that arise out of the core business of teaching and learning" (p. 150). This is precisely what Peter manages through his newsletter storytelling, using everyday incidents to combine the worlds of home and school in ways that are accessible to all.

Harris, Andrew-Powell and Goodall (2009) argue that the commitment of the principal, senior leadership team and/or senior leader is pivotal in moving the parental engagement agenda forward. The three key processes they advocate for this are the articulation of a clear vision, commitment, and an audit of existing practices. Again these processes are evident in the 2020VISION project at Southbridge School. This is indeed a challenging task and one that requires leadership actions that empower and inspire others to engage in reciprocal learning for the long term. Learning is the pulse behind Southbridge School, and to reiterate the words of Southworth, learning is dependent on the attributes of constant modelling, monitoring and dialogue for it to succeed.

Reflections for readers

The complexity and expansion of school leadership roles and responsibilities, particularly for school principals working in devolved educational settings, mean that more than ever principals need to make judicious decisions about how they can make the best use of their expertise and time so that their efforts enhance learning and teaching. An effective partnership with parents is crucial if the worlds of home and school are to connect. Therefore, leaders could usefully ask themselves:

- What can I do to ensure parental engagement is central to the school and its ways of working?
- What understanding do we share about the importance of parental engagement in learning?
- What strategies are the most effective for engaging parents with schools?
- How can schools ensure that parental engagement has a positive impact on students' learning?
- How can school principals retain parental engagement for learning in the school over time?

Suggested further reading

Allen, J. (2007). *Creating welcoming schools: A practical guide to home–school partnerships with diverse families*. New York, NY: Teachers College, Columbia University.

Bull, A., Brooking, K., & Campbell, R. (2008). *Successful home–school partnerships: Report to the Ministry of Education*. Wellington: NZCER Press.

Clinton, J., Hattie, J., & Dixon, R. (2007). *Evaluation of the Flaxmere project: When families learn the language of school*. Wellington: Ministry of Education.

Desforges, C., & Abouchaar, A. (2003). *The impact of parental involvement, parental support and family education on pupil achievement and adjustment: A literature review.* Research report No 433, Department of Education and Skills. Retrieved from http://www.dfes/gov.uk/research/data/uploadfiles/RR433.doc

MacBeath, J., & Dempster, N. (Eds.). (2009). *Connecting leadership and learning: Principles for practice.* London, UK: Routledge.

Timperley, H., & Robinson, V. (2002). *Partnership: Focusing the relationship on the task of school improvement.* Wellington: NZCER Press.

References

Bush, T. (2009). Leadership development and school improvement: Contemporary issues in leadership development. *Educational Review, 61*(4), 375–389.

Harris, A., & Muijs, D. (2005). *Improving schools through teacher leadership.* Maidenhead, Berkshire, UK: Open University Press.

Harris, A., Andrew-Powell, K., & Goodall, J. (2009). *Do parents know they matter? Raising achievement through parental engagement.* London, UK: Continuum.

Leithwood, K., Jantzi, D., & Steinbach, R. (1999). *Changing leadership for changing times.* Buckingham, UK: Open University Press.

Lovett, S., Verstappen, P., Clarke, M., & Gilmore, A. (2010, April). *2020VISION: How staff, children, and community combined to lead learning in a New Zealand primary school.* Paper presented to the New Zealand Educational Administration Leadership Society International Conference, University of Canterbury, Christchurch.

Organisation for Economic Co-operation and Development. (OECD). (2008). *Improving school leadership: Volume 1: Policy and practice.* OECD publishing. doi: 10.1787/9789264044715-en.

Robinson, V., Hohepa, M., & Lloyd, C. (2009). *School leadership and student outcomes: Identifying what works and why: Best evidence synthesis iteration.* Wellington: Ministry of Education.

Simons, H. (2009). *Case study research in practice.* London, UK: Sage.

Southworth, G. (2009). Learning-centred leadership. In B. Davies (Ed.), *The essentials of school leadership* (2nd ed., pp. 91–111). London, UK: Sage.

Acknowledgement

The author wishes to acknowledge the work of University of Canterbury researchers Michelle Clarke and Associate Professor Alison Gilmore who were the other members of the 2020VISION research team. Dissemination of this leadership case study from the 2020VISON project has been possible because of the funding granted by the Cognition Educational Research Institute.

CHAPTER 3

Leadership Located and Locatable

Hine Waitere

Georgina Kingi
Principal, St Joseph's Māori Girls' College (1987–present)

Shards of an enigma

The dimming lights catch the attention of an expectant audience—stilling animated conversations, stopping the waves of recognition, the nods of acknowledgement and the hugs that come with seeing old friends. Whānau[1] (extended family) and acquaintances settle back in their chairs and direct their attention to the stage. The school's reputation and the talents of its ex-pupils ensure the hall is full. Maisey Rika, the most recent graduate with music industry acclaim, takes the stage and confesses that, in spite of being comfortable performing in front of large audiences, both nationally and internationally, she is nervous tonight. Shifting her weight from one foot to the other, she confesses that the knot in the pit of her stomach is due to the fact that her old school principal, Miss Kingi, is in the audience.

The laughter in response to Maisey's tongue-in-cheek comment shows that it strikes a chord. It is obvious that she is not the only one Miss Kingi has had that effect on. In fact, what becomes clear through the course of our conversations is

---

1 A translation is supplied in brackets the first time Maori words and or phrases are used in this chapter.

that Georgina Kingi's diminutive frame belies her ability to punch well above her weight. Georgina, the principal of St Joseph's Māori Girls College, a decile 3 Catholic school in Greenmeadows, Taradale, leads a school that caters for approximately 230 Year 9 to 13 students, two-thirds of whom are boarders. As a principal of a relatively small Māori girls' boarding school, the breadth and depth of her impact is significant. It is clearly not constrained by school size or geographic location, nor is it limited by ethnicity, gender or religion.

In fact indicative of Georgina's mana were the responses her presence evoked amongst Maori men. On more than one occasion, chief executive officers, politicians, media personalities, lawyers, social activists, educators, university lecturers, researchers, doctors and 'radicals' alike, were observed to subtly shift their posture in her company or defer to her. Out of respect, these men would shuffle back in their chairs to sit a little more upright or, like Maisey, shift their weight to stand a little taller in her presence. Even though she has not taught or been the principal of any of these men, Miss Kingi's impact on this wider group is undeniable. It doesn't take much investigating to find out that behind the signifiers of respect is a complex web of relationships linking these men as cousins, brothers, sons, uncles, husbands, fathers and/or grandfathers of women who have attended or of girls who are currently attending what is commonly known as Saint Joe's. In fact, it is hard to think of a sector of society, in which Maori have a presence, that Georgina has not touched, through the daughters, granddaughters, sisters, aunties, mothers, wives, and grandmothers she has taught. Georgina, a past pupil of the school, never trained as a teacher. In 1969 Sister Mary Katarina (herself an old girl) asked Georgina to relieve for her so that she could go on sabbatical. The position was only to be for 3 months. Although Georgina did not see this as a particularly auspicious moment, Sister Katarina never returned to the school and Georgina has never left. She moved from assistant teacher (1969–1974) to head of department of Māori Studies (1974–1985). Her role as head of department overlapped with her contribution to the senior management team (1983–1985). In 1985, after encouragement from whakapapa and kaupapa-based whānau, Georgina became deputy principal, before assuming her current role as principal in 1987.

Her notion of excellence weaves together cultural identity, fundamental values (Māori and Catholic) and a commitment to high academic achievement based on an unwavering belief in each girl's potential

Having spent her entire career at the one school has never dampened Georgina's passion for teaching, nor her demand for excellence. Her notion of excellence weaves together cultural identity, fundamental values (Māori and Catholic) and a commitment to high academic achievement based on an unwavering belief in each girl's potential. Georgina will tell you that she won her senior positions simply because there was nobody else to fill these roles. However, as a recipient of the Queen's Service Order (awarded in 2004 for community contribution) and the Benemerenti Medal (awarded by Pope Benedict in 2006 for service to Catholic education, the church, family and community), one might reasonably suspect a very different story to the self-effacing view Georgina has of her own achievements.

This chapter provides an insight into an enigma, a woman who will tell you without malice or disrespect that she was "Maori before she was Catholic." She will also claim that while the girls understand that she may be *a witch to them*, she will add with conviction that they also understand she is prepared to be *a bitch for them*. As forthright and as unapologetic as Georgina is in her convictions about the school, her leadership is grounded in a socio-historical context that simultaneously shapes and is shaped by her. Later in the chapter, our discussion will focus on the interplay between Georgina's educational visions for the girls and the impact the socio-cultural context has on Georgina's approach to transformation. Before this, two themes are explored which emerged out of our conversations that focus on purposeful relationships and the notion of enduring struggles.

Purposeful relationships

A biting wind marks our arrival in Dunedin. The temperature helps explain the bulge in Georgina's handbag, stressed by tights destined for the legs of past pupils studying at Otago University. It does not occur to me to ask if the sizes are right. She knows which girls are there, what they are studying, who has changed programmes and whether or not she agrees with such shifts. They meet for lunch and a cell phone rings—a kuia (grandmother) has died. A mokopuna (grandchild) is dumbstruck: how is this kid getting back up north? Georgina picks up the phone and takes control. She knows who, she knows what, she knows where ... she knows.

Georgina will tell you that though relationships are the fundamental building blocks of Māori communities and their engagement in education, she is equally adamant that the relationships developed at school need to be purposeful and interdependent. The girls in Dunedin understand this principle. They know that being treated to lunch is derived from a real concern for their well-being. They also know that Georgina's interest does not stop with their physical welfare. They are aware there is an expectation regarding their academic performance and that they will be made to account for their progress. They will also be asked about the courses they are doing and their merit. They will be probed about challenges confronted and what they are doing to resolve them. The girls will be asked what they are doing to support each other. Georgina will also ask about girls who are not at lunch. She expects the girls to work as individuals but to support each other. She knows these girls well and they know her. Georgina embodies the school motto, "I o mahi katoa mahia: Whatever work you do, do it well."

Georgina spends a lot of time thinking and talking about relationships, both culturally and pedagogically. She is not interested in laissez-faire relationships—quite the opposite. They must be purposeful relationships that emerge out of the school's ability to recognise community aspirations and an ability to respond in culturally responsive ways. Creating an institutional culture that recognises and values the cultural backgrounds of the girls is key to success as Georgina sees it.

The relationships developed at school need to be purposeful and interdependent

With the increased focus on relationships in teaching and learning she is careful to distinguish between relationships where the students are made to simply feel good and relationships that are based on fundamental respect and an unwavering belief in each girl's competence and capability. Working in the face of a depressing array of educational statistics, Georgina sees the school working in opposition to hegemonic norms about race, gender, class and the debilitating pathologies associated with each. She refuses to accept any attempt from those around her to use stereotypical assumptions about the girls as a reason to abdicate staff responsibility to helping them achieve their potential.

Translating her vision for positive educational outcomes into action, Georgina explicitly challenges staff to promote and engage students in educationally demanding experiences and opportunities. Quick to pick up on shifts, in a recent prize-giving speech Georgina remarked that with the staff, students and whānau collectively stepping up, everyone needed to be congratulated for the breadth of educational opportunities offered and taken up by the girls. Prominent among the successes were the growing number of girls entering scholarship in subjects such as English, Geography, History and Classical Studies; more senior students being able to simultaneously enrol in te reo Māori (Māori language) courses offered by Massey University; and the number of girls continuing to perform well in the highly competitive regional and national Manu Korero speech competitions.

On the back of a number of firsts coming from St Joseph's, such as the first female Māori engineer and the first female Māori forensic scientist, normalising success in multiple areas sends the important message that being Māori provides a strong platform on which success is built and from which any aspiration can be launched. The girls sitting at lunch in a Dunedin café know that the relationship developed in school does not end when they walk out of the school gate at the end of secondary school; it simply marks the transition from being a current student to being an old girl.

Comparing St Joseph's academic achievements against national averages for Māori and the student population in general shows the extent to which the girls' accomplishments stand out against a backdrop of statistics that reflect the under-realisation of Māori potential. For example, in 2009 100 percent of St Joseph's students achieved NCEA Level 1, 100 percent achieved NCEA Level 2, and 89 percent were awarded NCEA Level 3. Compared with Māori and European national averages, sitting at 53 percent and 79 percent for Level 1 respectively, 62 percent and 81 percent for Level 2, and 52 percent and 74 percent for Level 3, St Joseph's students are shown to perform well. Comparing these academic results with schools of a similar decile ranking further highlights the school's achievements.

Successes in academic achievement have not occurred by chance. They emerge out of a socio-historical context that has required a concerted and sustained effort to challenge assumptions about student capability, processes and practices that has, at times, put Georgina at odds with other people. The push for purposeful, educative, in-school relationships in the face of significant disparities explains the characterisation of Georgina as "the witch." Georgina knows how she is read; she acknowledges the caricature created by students, knowing that pushing for better performance is part of her strategy to increase the girls' life chances and life choices.

This characterisation is echoed in Robinson, Hohepa and Lloyd's (2009) best evidence synthesis, where the writers suggest that the quality of leader–staff relationships is not necessarily predictive of the quality of student outcomes. This is because, they argue, there is more to educational leadership than building collegial teams, establishing a loyal and cohesive staff, and developing a shared and inspirational vision. Educational leadership is also about focusing such relationships in purposeful ways; on pedagogical work in the classroom.

Enduring struggles

The wānanga (meeting) is over. The team is busy loading vehicles. A young woman carrying a child on her hip arrives looking for Miss Kingi. She wants to take Georgina to the airport. Of course Georgina could come with any of us. We are, after all, going to the same place, but who would miss an opportunity to catch up with a past pupil? It's hot. The child fights mum's attempts to restrain him in his car seat. He bellows his objection, punches the air with his little fists and arches his back, fighting against unyielding seatbelts. A harried young mum changes gear and tyres crunch metal on the loose gravel driveway. As the car begins to move, Georgina winds down the window and comments, "See. I even have this effect on the next generation!"

Georgina is no stranger to struggle. In fact, there are many who would describe her as a battler. In the course of her principal journey, Georgina has led St Joseph's through a raft of changes. These include the educational reforms of the eighties and nineties and the transition from solely boarding to accepting day students in order to embrace local iwi. There have also been significant changes in curricula, shifts in assessment with regard to what knowledge is valued and how it is credentialed, and external monitoring of in-school processes and practices. Through being forced to balance the overlapping wants, needs and aspirations of different groups within the school, Georgina has had to negotiate an educational terrain in which adopting, adapting and, at times, resisting the wants of some and the needs of others has placed her at odds with many.

At times the struggle has been an in-school battle, where Georgina has found herself in contention with students who have internalised hegemonic assumptions about their own capability as individuals and as Māori. Her response has been to confront stereotypes by challenging the girls to excel in the face of self-doubt. In these moments she recognises that cajoling, pushing and prodding accentuate her tough reputation. There have also been occasions when the demand for positive student outcomes has created tensions with teachers, who, at times, have been equally influenced by deficit thinking about the capability of individual students. Her demand for excellence encompasses staff (academic, administrative, boarding) and students. She understands that they are all interconnected. This interdependent relationship recognises that students reach their potential through sound, culturally cognisant pedagogical interactions derived from an understanding of the context in which teaching and learning occur.

To say that Georgina's struggles are contained within the school gates, however, belies the breadth of relationships she has in mind when she thinks about these girls (and the kuia and koroua (male and female forbears) she sees reflected in the faces of the girls). Often it is seeing the older generation that fuels her determination to achieve her educational vision, one she believes is held by the Maori whānau who send their girls to St Joseph's.

As any account of her career will show, Georgina has consistently stood by her convictions. At times this has pitted her against Child, Youth and Family services, put her at odds with the Education Review Office, and seen her challenge teacher unions, the church and, on different occasions, whānau as well. Although the groups listed have differed in their views regarding practices or protocols, none would question Georgina's commitment to the students and the school. Georgina has a determination and an unapologetic approach to raising Māori student achievement. In spite of her reluctance to talk about herself, she clearly has a strong sense of her own agency. She has not argued or fought with these groups all at once, nor does she sit in opposition to them all of the time. However, she has struggled with and against them enough times to have earned a reputation for being a tough, forthright woman whose assertive leadership style has her recognised as a force to be reckoned with as she works to support the girls in her school.

> *As any account of her career will show, Georgina has consistently stood by her convictions*

Context matters

> Let my community judge me. When I look at these girls, it is not their faces I see. Often, it is the faces of their kuia and koroua. When you see the girls this way, it brings with it a whole lot of layers of accountability. To teach in a place like this, you have to wrap the community around you. When you work here, you better be prepared to be judged, judged by your community, by whānau (family) and whānau whānui (extended family). (Georgina Kingi, 2010)

Few contemporary studies on educational leadership would avoid the dynamic interplay between context and the way leadership plays out. The current interest in context is underpinned by the knowledge that leadership does not occur in a vacuum, abstracted from the macro and micro forces that help to shape those who lead. Certainly Georgina as a Māori woman working in a Māori boarding school recognises the importance of context and its fundamental impact on her role as a transformative leader. In fact, striving to provide an insight into Georgina's experience as a principal and what drives her, it is difficult to separate what she does from who she is and the geo-political context in which she sees herself.

Georgina's story is important for a number of reasons, particularly when educational leaders, drawn from diverse backgrounds, search for normative entry points into leadership discussions that neither see Maori women leading as typical nor work to normalise what they do. Georgina's story raises more questions than it answers about leadership in both macro and micro contexts, where different cultural worlds not only meet but often confront each other. Leading within a church-based, indigenous, all girls boarding school, Georgina traverses a context not only imbued with colonial legacies and assumptions about race, gender and spirituality, but she also leads in a context influenced by contemporary forces that produce stereotypical assumptions about difference. The politics in Aotearoa New Zealand is nowhere more evident than in the history of boarding schools established to educate indigenous students, which is the context in which Georgina leads.

She also leads in a context influenced by contemporary forces that produce stereotypical assumptions about difference

Boarding schools for indigenous children, such as St Joseph's, have a particular place in educational history. As with mainstream education, the separate educational provision for indigenous (aboriginal, first nations) peoples extends beyond the shores of Aotearoa New Zealand. Indigenous boarding schools were generally established as a way of dealing with the diversity colonialists encountered in native populations. Contrary to Georgina's educational goals for the girls at St Joseph's the historical purpose of boarding or residential schools was to expunge difference by assimilating indigenous pupils into the dominant society (Jenkins and Matthews 1998; Barrington and Beaglehole, 1974). They were not seen as appropriate places for indigenous peoples to lead (Jenkins and Matthews 1998). These schools, frequently administered by Christian missions, were created with the express purpose of Christianising indigenous peoples, particularly in Latin America, North America, the Arctic and the Pacific (Smith, 2009). In Aotearoa New Zealand, Māori boarding schools were set up with the express purpose of civilising and assimilating the natives by removing children from "the demoralising influences of their papa kāinga (villages)" (Barrington and Beaglehole, 1974).

Comparing boarding schools for Māori in Aotearoa New Zealand with similar schools in other countries helps map the context in which Georgina leads. The historical background is not intended to provoke consternation. What is important is that Māori boarding schools, established out of the same colonial epoch, have had a different genesis to mainstream schools. Equally, there are stories to be told about educational leadership that explain why the provision took a different path in Aotearoa New Zealand to elsewhere. It is significant that leading in this context has normalised the critical need to struggle for equitable educational provision. It also provides a catalyst for Georgina's strong, forthright and sometimes defiant character. Georgina is often confronted by discourses and discursive practices that underpin debilitating norms. She is also privy to the hopes and aspirations of whānau for their children. In this way, Georgina understands both similarity and difference.

In the context where those external to the group assume sameness, Georgina recognises that intra-culturally she is located and locatable by a framework that values her Ngāti Awa (Awa tribe) and Ngāti Pukekotanga (cultural values and beliefs of the Pukeko tribe). It is within this framework that difference is also privileged. Thus within St Joseph's she does not just see *sameness*. In fact, through the images of kuia and koroua seen in the more youthful faces of the girls at St Joseph's, Georgina is reminded of rich and sometimes traumatic variances associated with the differential impact of colonisation on tribal groups that lead to land loss for some, relocation for others and a stripping of an economic, social, cultural and linguistic legacy for others. Locating individuals within collectives, without sacrificing the former for the latter, she operates in a context in which girls are drawn from diverse iwi, class, regional and gendered Māori realities. Georgina's knowledge of, and engagement in, Māori communities contributes to shaping the form and function of her leadership. Remembering the geo-political and multi-generational context that is embodied in, and wrapped around, the girls helps Georgina to locate the "witch" and "bitch" characters that she candidly refers to.

It is somewhat ironic that Māori boarding schools, initially set up to limit educational offerings, currently work in opposition to the intent of their establishment. When measured against schools' ability to deliver educational outcomes *for* Māori, St Joseph's enjoys national success. This is supported by educational policies such as Ka Hikitia (Ministry of Education, 2008), which aspires to have Māori students enjoying educational outcomes *as* Māori.

Smith (2003) writing about transformative aspirations in the context of Māori leadership identifies five critical sites of struggle that help to illustrate Georgina's own transformative aspirations. First, he suggests there is a need to understand and respond to the unhelpful division between indigenous communities and formalised, educational institutional contexts. For Georgina, understanding the impact of distrust that still exists within Māori communities in relation to access, participation and educational success underpins her push to educate beyond the self-fulfilling cycle of educational underachievement and the consequent socioeconomic realities Maori experience. Second, as Smith (2003) maintains, there is a need to understand

and respond to the new formations of colonisation. For Georgina, this is evident in her resistance to ongoing hegemonies about deviance. Third, Smith argues that achieving educational change is built on the need to understand and respond to the politics of distraction, whereby initiatives that keep indigenous people busy with surface change prevent engagement with the deeper structural issues that need to be addressed in order to achieve Māori educational aspirations.

Fourth, in keeping with general conceptions of transformational theory, there is a need to have a vision of what is being struggled for. The transformative vision Georgina holds on to relates to the need to reclaim the validity and legitimacy of reo Māori, knowledge and culture. Finally, there is a need to engage with the state, and to encourage the state to work for indigenous interests as well. For Georgina, this is why the struggle is multi-faceted and located in multiple spaces.

Conclusion

Whether I used a feminist analysis or a Māori cultural paradigm, getting Georgina to focus on herself was difficult. She would constantly sidestep the focus on her and, with a dismissive wave of a hand, move on to other educational matters. In discussions of her personal traits and characteristics I was simply redirected to Ngāti Pukeko kaumātua (tribal elders) to extend that aspect of the conversation—much like someone researching other principals might be directed to a library to track the development of a line of enquiry. Not surprisingly, her position and responses can also be explained through other cultural precepts that value humility, and the preference for letting actions speak for themselves. Georgina's reflections, though constantly self-effacing, are clearly located within her understanding of an educational context where she not only reads others but is also aware of how they read her.

As this chapter draws to a close, aware that there is so much more to be said about Georgina I find myself reflecting on my own years as a pupil of a Māori girls' boarding school and on the nature of schooling in Aotearoa New Zealand. Although I accept total responsibility for what I have written and for any errors or omissions I nevertheless find myself also shifting my weight in my chair wondering ... would Miss Kingi approve?

Reflections for readers

As Zigarmi, Fowler and Lyles (2005) point out, a multitude of leadership books treat leadership as if "one size fits all", as if leadership skills were silver bullets ready to be applied across any circumstance. Certainly Georgina's experience suggests that leadership is situated in a local context, mediated by interdependent relationships that mean one's leadership does not play out in a vacuum. Generic leadership characteristics may expunge context, but the leadership challenges Georgina faces are always contextual, always situated with particular people, with specific circumstances and histories.

Georgina's story reflects Mertz and McNeely's (1998) claim that there is a need for a multidimensional approach to understanding leadership. They call for methods that examine context, ethnicity, gender and other factors when conducting research on leadership style. A decade on, however, it is still rare to find studies that investigate the impact of ethnicity, gender and culture as overlapping socio-cultural influences on the context in which one leads. The paucity of research literature that examines indigenous leadership situated within a colonial context makes it difficult to map Georgina's experience of leadership in the canon. For example, if feminist analyses are correct in their claims that prejudices, beliefs and habits have made it virtually impossible for women to hold leadership positions, then the glass ceilings made visible by feminist critique are surely double glazed by gendered and race-based assumptions about indigenous women.

The point is that we do not have a current framework within existing theory to decipher the effect that colonial histories have on indigenous women leaders in mainstream educational contexts. Georgina's struggle to transform social conditions, structures, processes and practices often requires her to work in the face of hegemonic forces as she strives to realise a contrary vision. Georgina's story appears located, specific and contextually muddied in a canon that sets itself up as universal, neutral and, therefore, equally applicable to all.

Reflective questions that arise from this chapter:
- Georgina locates herself within a particularised context with a clear focus on Māori achievement. Does the context she is talking about only have relevance for educational institutions where there are large Māori student populations? Or is the struggle for improved educational outcomes for Māori a national issue?
- Georgina talks about leadership that is prepared to work against the grain, against 'normalised' beliefs about the 'lack' of Māori student ability and capability that works to undermine Māori students achieving their potential. What do the educational professionals and support staff, in your workplace, know about the Maori students and community in your school or centre? How does this help you engage with Māori and with Māori knowledge?
- What would a cycle of inquiry, based on getting to know your Māori community, look like? Who would be involved in the inquiry? What data would you want to collect?

- There is a strong undercurrent of intersecting values in this narrative. What opportunities do we create to talk about converging values in our workplaces?

Suggested further reading

Ashcroft, B., Griffiths, G., & Tiffin, H. (2009). *Post-colonial studies: The key concepts*. London, UK: Routledge.

Klenke, K. (1996). *Women and leadership: A contextual perspective*. Dordrecht, The Netherlands: Springer.

Wurtzel, E. (1999). *Bitch: In praise of difficult women*. New York USA: Knopf Doubleday Publishing.

References

Barrington, J., & Beaglehole, T. (1974). *Maori schools in a changing society: An historical review*. Wellington: New Zealand Council for Educational Research.

Jenkins K., & Matthews, K. M. (1998) Knowing their place: The political socialisation of Maori women in New Zealand through schooling policy and practice, 1867-1969. *Women's History Review*, 7(1), 85-105.

Mertz, N., & McNeely, S. R. (1998). Women on the job: A study of female high school principals. *Education Administration Quarterly*, 34(2), 196–222.

Ministry of Education. (2008). *Ka hikitia: Managing for success: The Māori education strategy*. Wellington: Author.

Robinson, V., Hohepa, M., & Lloyd, C. (2009). *School leadership and student outcomes: Identifying what works and why: Best evidence synthesis iteration*. Wellington: Ministry of Education.

Smith, A. (2009, May). *Report on indigenous peoples boarding schools for the Secretariat of the United Nations Permanent Forum on Indigenous Issues*, eighth session, New York.

Smith, G. H. (2003, October). *Indigenous struggle for the transformation of education and schooling*. Keynote Address to the Alaskan Federation of Natives (AFN) Convention, Anchorage, AK.

Zigarmi, D., Fowler, S., & Lyles, D. (2005). Context: The Rosetta stone of leadership. *Leader to Leader Institute*, *38*, Autumn, 37–44.

CHAPTER 4

Philosophical Leadership: Mike's Story

Jeremy Kedian

Mike Sutton
Principal, Patetonga School (1977–1980)
Principal, Kaiaua School (1980–1985)
Principal, St Patrick's Catholic School, Te Awamutu (1986–1994)
Principal, Leamington Primary School (1995–2001)
Principal, Nawton School (2001–2008)
Principal, Rototuna Primary School (2008–present)

Introduction

This narrative is unashamedly part of Mike's story of developing as a leader. It is about Mike's leadership philosophy, his philosophy of student learning and student-centredness, and his professional practice as a leader. It includes the clear interaction of reflection, meta-reflection, current theory, values and practice as they combine to develop a philosophy that guides his personal practice. At all times during this research project Mike was an active participant, which is in itself a reflection of his philosophy. In telling his story I have attempted to remain true to his purpose by using his words, his language and his ideas.

As will become clear, Mike's focus is on student learning and achievement, and how these can best be supported. To achieve this he supports his staff in various ways, builds capacity, develops dispositions and builds relationships. He sees the value of trust, and of sharing his leadership with others in the school. Mike leads from the front—and from behind. He believes that the stories of the other leaders in his school are also important because they have the potential to influence their professional practice long into the future.

The beginning

Having been a principal for over 30 years, Mike has served as a principal under both the centralised and the decentralised New Zealand education systems. He began his career in principalship when he was appointed to a small, two-teacher rural primary school in a dairy farming area. He later moved to a school in a seaside fishing settlement. After a few years he moved to a Catholic integrated school. With the next step in his career he went back into the state-funded mainstream, as principal of a decile 3 school.[1] This was the first principalship in which he had contact with bilingual education. From there Mike moved to a larger decile 2 school of 550 children. This provided a further challenge in that it had six total immersion (te reo Māori) and two bilingual classes, with the rest of the school being taught in English.

These last three schools provided challenging professional contexts as well as important professional learning opportunities. Leadership of these three schools contributed to Mike's development as a principal, in that they gave him a breadth of understanding of the importance of ethnic and organisational culture and of the cross-pollination of ideas. Mike saw the need for developing a personal and professional values base that incorporates the social, cultural and learning needs of multiple groups.

Mike saw the need for developing a personal and professional values base that incorporates the social, cultural and learning needs of multiple groups

Mike then branched out into what he refers to as "new territory" by accepting an appointment to a 750-student, decile 10 school—the highest possible socio-economic rating. At the time the school was relatively new; Mike was its second principal and was appointed in its seventh year. Accordingly, the school was still growing and developing an identity and place in the community.

A clear challenge to Mike as the school's second principal was to test and apply his leadership philosophy, values and strategies. He acknowledges that a key aspect of doing this was to ensure that his leadership strategies were based on the needs of the school rather than the fact he had used them successfully in previous

---

1 Decile refers to a rating given by the Ministry of Education that reflects the socio-economic level of the majority of families in the school. This figure, on a scale of 1 to 10 (where 10 is the highest), determines the level of government funding per student to the school.

institutions. This required him to develop new and different strategies, to frequently move out of the comfort zone created by his past experiences, and to challenge his own leadership beliefs and those of other leaders around him.

Personal professional learning

During his fourth principalship Mike attended a series of professional learning programmes. This further stimulated his interest in the theory and practice of leadership, to the extent that he embarked on an Educational Leadership degree. This allowed him to formalise his learning in leadership and to increase his competence and confidence when encountering new and unusual contexts and issues. Importantly, it gave him the ability to begin to theorise about his professional practice in a meaningful way. He reflects on this period of formal study:

> I became more rounded as an educator and leader ... I understood better the organisational systems and the theory behind why we do what we do. I understood why we work with teachers the way we do and why we used coaching as an important way to develop teachers.

Mike has other specific beliefs about professional learning. One important one is that principals need to model personal professional learning. Rather than simply talk about the importance of professional learning, the staff need to see it happening. Another is the need for the principal to be involved in the professional learning planned for the staff. Mike believes that if it is important enough to take up valuable staff time, then it is important enough for the principal to participate fully. This active participation is a relentless focus for him.

Principals need to model personal professional learning

Developing excellence and effectiveness

Modelling, in Mike's view, is a crucial way of developing leadership in the school. Staff need to see the principal engaging with leadership theory and literature, reflecting on personal leadership practice, engaging in dialogue about leadership and developing a leadership network outside of the school. These show the staff that leadership is not so much a status as an opportunity to serve the needs of the school—a way of being.

Modelling leadership practice involves elements of risk-taking. School leaders often applaud risk-taking as a concept but are reluctant to see it happen in practice. It is important to Mike that he not only takes risks but is seen to be taking risks. One area of risk he describes is giving power and authority to a teacher to complete a particular project when, as leader, you are not certain they are ready to meet the challenge. To maximise the likelihood of success he often spends time with teachers in this context and works through various scenarios with them. This requires him to act in a mentoring role and to spend time with his staff in dialogue and joint reflection. This might include offering readings (for example, on holding difficult conversations) and other resources. He says it is important to "do this in order to help staff to build a picture, to visualize what certain situations are going to look like."

School leaders often applaud risk taking as a concept but are reluctant to see it happen in practice

Mike describes risk-taking as a constructive disposition. At times it is reactive, but it is more likely to be proactive, in that risk-taking is future-focused and relies on creativity rather than precedent. Risk-taking also promotes individuality and values the essence of individual experiences and knowledge. Mike acknowledges that while his leadership team of 10 staff share common values, they also each have their own values. He appreciates this and believes that differences in values introduce a dimension of leadership thinking that is unlikely to prevail where a particular set of values dominates. These differences, he claims, allow personalities, values and beliefs to emerge and contribute to the broader picture. Furthermore, he suggests that this is more likely to develop people who:

> think outside of the square, who will challenge one another's thinking because challenge is not disrespect or disbelief but rather a process of seeking best outcomes—it's trying to clarify situations. A hierarchy of values and structures will tend to diminish people's ability to make creative decisions ... [and so] reducing hierarchy and encouraging risk-taking leads to better outcomes for students.

A useful strategy Mike uses is to develop reflective practice in individuals as well as the leadership team. He argues that reflexivity is one of his core strengths and dispositions. For Mike, reflection occurs before and after decisions and processes or events. He will model reflective practice before an event to demonstrate forms of leadership that produce the best outcomes. In contrast, post-event reflection represents a form of analysis and meta-reflection. In this case, he will reflect on how the process turned out and the steps that were involved. Rather than knowing, he begins with a process of wondering. For example, if he had ignored the context and looked solely at the event, might he have strategised and facilitated the process in a different way? If he had applied different values, would the outcome have been different? What does a particular event mean? How can it be explained? What might the meaning and explanations imply for the future? These questions are central to his reflective practice.

Leadership perspectives and strategies

Mike sees school leadership as a multi-faceted, layered concept comprising systemic thinking, a shared vision and relationships.

Building trusting relationships

In Mike's opinion, relationships are a key to successful leadership. They include human relationships with the community, teachers, students and other stakeholders. They also include organisational relationships, which mainly refer to systems within the school and to government agencies. Mike acknowledges that boundaries within the school and between people can be made more permeable and minimised by the development of functional relationships. This is supported by his leadership structure, which has two deputy principals who are not tagged to particular areas of the school and are expected to work across the organisation, utilising their skills in the best way for the team. These relationships, he claims, acknowledge the ebb and flow of the organisation of the school. He sees relationships as the basis of organisational trust.

As an experienced leader he believes that the process of building trusting relationships requires the leader to be vulnerable at times, "to admit when you don't know" and to seek advice and support. This notion applies to all leaders in the school, including teachers. This could be because a willingness to display vulnerability is an acknowledgement of a culture of trust. When this occurs, the culture of the school begins to change in not-so-subtle ways, with a high trust culture emerging as a powerful underpinning of staff and student learning. Members of the school no longer fear one another, students trust their teachers to do the best for them, teachers trust students to take responsibility for their own learning, and all members trust that each will do what they say they will.

> *As an experienced leader he believes that the process of building trusting relationships requires the leader to be vulnerable at times, "to admit when you don't know" and to seek advice and support*

Distributing leadership

Equally central to Mike's philosophy of leadership is the requirement of *distributed* or *shared* leadership. In his words, "One of the logical things that comes out of all of this is that if you truly believe in relationships and you truly believe in developing trust, then you have to believe in distributed leadership." Distributed leadership, in his understanding, is essentially a school-wide phenomenon in which leadership becomes the responsibility of all rather than the domain of an élite. If it takes place in a culture of high trust, leadership becomes pervasive and leaders emerge where leadership is required. This means that leadership is relational, contextualised, interdisciplinary, located and authentic.

Mike acknowledges that distributing leadership introduces a very real element of vulnerability. In most education systems the principal is the one who is ultimately accountable. However, with distributed leadership the principal accepts being externally accountable for work over which she or he has no real control. This context of accountability leads to a vulnerability for the principal that is not necessarily self-evident. Mike addresses this issue by acknowledging that powerful relationships within a high-trust model create a context in which staff, as leaders, have easy access to critical peers who act as a sounding board for projects. In addition, appropriate safety mechanisms can be developed that prevent project failure while maximising teachers' leadership opportunities. There are risks inherent in this level of distributed leadership, as Mike acknowledges, but the one non-negotiable requirement for the development of leadership ability is the opportunity to lead.

Contextual awareness

Effectiveness is contextual, and Mike expresses a deep concern about the potential for regression when a new principal is appointed to a school. He fears that new principals tend to re-create what they have already experienced rather than altering their leadership to suit the different context. He believes that a common error of new principals is to refer to activities "at my last school", as though they are some form of touchstone or basis for decision making. This, he suggests, could be indicative of an inability to let go of previous baggage rather than useful experience. He also suggests that it is inadvisable to "turn a school upside down when you first walk in", because this tends to invalidate the work or processes that have gone on before. Such a move can undermine the motivation of existing staff and leaders, and is potentially a cultural toxin.

Mike believes that a far better approach to taking on a new principalship is to devote time to developing relationships and asking questions about the processes at the school, their origins and utility. He describes this as follows:

> With the distributive leadership approach that I prefer … I worked for a long time with relationships, and then talking about processes and activities with questions like: So why is that job so big?—and how can we support that teacher or that leader to be more effective? People began to realise through the questioning and being asked to reflect that maybe some of the jobs were too big. So it created an environment where people asked: '…is there a different way of doing these things?'

This enquiring, reflective approach serves as a model for distributed leadership by encouraging all staff to ask the hard questions that refocus the organisation's attention on student learning. This could be perceived as a way of introducing teaching staff to leadership decision making, where decisions are based on moral purpose and the core intent of the organisation, rather than any potential sectoral advantage within the school.

Leadership strategies for student learning

Mike firmly believes that improving levels of student learning is essentially an exercise in pedagogic focus and change. He is adamant that as the principal of a large school, he alone cannot bring about the required change. It requires commitment from all the staff, which, he says, brings him back to the idea of trust.

Partnerships and coaching

To address the issue of pedagogic change in an inclusive way, Mike introduced the notion of critical partnerships and coaching. One of the main vehicles he has employed is classroom visits, and the leadership team has also developed a process of classroom observations. To change pedagogy, a teacher needs appropriate, in-depth feedback on their own professional practice. This is developed on the basis of triangulated data.

In the first instance, the teacher and leadership team have access to student learning data from multiple student achievement tests, observations and anecdotal data. Then a coaching colleague is invited to spend time observing in the classroom. The observer begins by meeting with the teacher to discuss the teacher's pedagogic philosophy and strategies. By the time the first observation takes place, the observer is aware of the teacher's professional context as well as the classroom learning culture. As a result, the observations are purposeful and carefully structured.

> *To change pedagogy, a teacher needs appropriate, in-depth feedback on their own professional practice*

Finally, the observer draws on the student voice by asking simple questions such as "What was our lesson about today?", "What do you think you are learning?", "Why are you learning this today?", "How will you know when you have learnt this?" and "How does your teacher help you to…?". These simple questions offer crucial feedback to teachers regarding their teaching activities, student learning and pathways for future learning. The student voice also often enables the coach/observer to introduce alternative perspectives that challenge the teacher's view of the lesson. And just as the teachers may co-construct when working with a critical peer, the observers, as critical peers, also have the opportunity to discuss their observations and impending feedback with Mike or another leader.

Mike links this to West-Burnham's (2009) distinction between immature and mature leadership. He contends that as relationships improve and trust grows, the degree of open dialogue improves to the point where teachers are able to move from dependence to inter-dependence as professionals. As a result, the staff begin to see classroom visits by colleagues as a powerful opportunity for personal professional growth rather than a somewhat threatening administrative duty to be tolerated. Rather than being evaluative, these classroom visits offer Mike an opportunity to engage in processes of teaching and learning, to observe what teachers do to facilitate learning, and to demonstrate clearly that he values what teachers do. Part of this philosophy is based on a critical early experience he had as a first- and second-year teacher:

> My principal invited me to have lunch with him once a week. As we ate our sandwiches he would ask questions such as: 'Tell me about your reading programme, or have you thought about …' and other questions that forced me to explore my practice. Then he would offer very, very rich, constructive feedback and ideas about alternative strategies. Then he would say, 'Try it for a week or two and I'll come and have a look.'

Leadership presence

Mike believes that leaders should have a "presence." For a start, they should be present as frequently as possible in classrooms to observe students' learning. A by-product of this is that it provides an opportunity to interact at a highly professional level with classroom teachers. He is concerned that, in New Zealand, as in many other Western countries, there appears to be an imperative for principals to be out of the classroom. Mike's core belief is that the converse is true.

Leaders should also have a presence in the sense that they have credibility and stature in the eyes of the school community. It is clear from his professional practice that Mike has a high level of credibility, both inside and outside of his school. This credibility, Mike argues, stems from an observed level of excellence and understanding in matters concerning curriculum and pedagogy. It is not sufficient for principals to be organisational leaders. They also need to be leaders of learning. Their level of credibility, he contends, resides in staff perceptions of the principal's ability to work effectively as a curriculum and classroom leader, a leader of learning, a leader of staff and a leader of organisational direction.

This credibility, Mike argues, stems from an observed level of excellence and understanding in matters concerning curriculum and pedagogy

Challenges and dilemmas

Like most other principals, Mike faces challenges and dilemmas that create tensions. In the New Zealand decentralised context he sees conflicts arising between national policy and classroom activities. Mike believes that a principal needs to be pragmatic at times. The introduction of the controversial national standards in New Zealand is a good example of this approach. He feels that the concept has some potential and is better than the option of national testing. His view is that it is best to work from the inside and influence policy and the way the system can work. In this case, the introduction of the standards showed up a gap in how his staff made decisions about learning that enabled the leadership team to develop professional learning opportunities to best meet the needs of the school.

Teacher motivation and learning is another focus of Mike's leadership. Teachers generally want to be the best they can and want their students to achieve the same. A principal needs to capitalise on this and promote and show that the changes being introduced will contribute to teacher and student learning. In doing this, though, Mike believes that principals need to manage teacher workload, and that change also needs to address this major issue. He suggests that although schools are adept at adding teacher functions and duties, they usually do so without looking at the existing responsibilities they might replace.

One of the greatest challenges Mike faces is improving the level of student achievement and learning. These are not necessarily synonymous, as achieving both requires a holistic approach. Mike comments that "There is a danger in our profession that everything is based on data or statistics. However, I think that anecdotal, qualitative data based on observations creates another dimension of understanding." Mike has a strong belief that effective principals understand the workings of the whole school. He says:

> *There is a danger in our profession that everything is based on data or statistics*

> After a few years of teaching, I decided that it was probably time to develop my skills a little more and so I actively applied for, and won, a position that nowadays would be called AP [Assistant Principal] of Junior Classes. I did this because I needed to find out how children learned as five and six-year-olds.

This was clearly an important decision, because he now reports the benefits of his ability to relate to what happens in the junior part of the school. As teacher, observer or coach Mike remains comfortable in new entrant or Year 1 classes as a consequence of his earlier experiences. He is also able to contribute knowledgably and credibly to dialogue on activities in junior phases of the school. This allows him to develop and share a broad perspective on the learning needs of students as they grow and progress through their primary school years.

Conclusion

As a member of a principal cluster Mike attempts to share as much as possible. His professional values and beliefs require him to support other people as they grow as leaders in their schools and to seek out learning opportunities from other members of his professional community. He has contributed to professional learning programmes in at least four other countries and sees this as a powerful contributor to his own professional learning. This learning involves a combination of non-formal, enquiry-based programmes, along with formal elements such as his enrolment in a doctoral programme. He sees formal study not as an arduous task but what he describes as "probably the icing on the cake that has had the biggest effect on my career in the last fifteen years." Mike is emphatic that formal and non-formal learning create opportunities for professional sharing among peers. Although he is concerned that a devolved system may work against this professional sharing, he has made it part of his professional practice to ensure that collaborative and collegial opportunities continue.

Mike is motivated by the desire to continue to grow as a principal, leader and learner. He believes there is a need to continue to grow the leadership within the school and, ultimately, the profession:

> We need to grow the leaders of today and tomorrow so that this wonderful profession can continue to evolve. I also continue to enjoy the debate about teaching and learning, and the challenges of leadership. I believe that I need to continue to grow teachers and teaching that is sustainable so there is a huge need to provide quality, focused professional learning.

Reflections for readers

Mike's practice is underpinned by a clear and firm philosophy. He argues that it is this philosophy that has led him to a place in his professional practice where he is considered highly effective. Drawing on the work of Giles (2008), Buber (2002), West-Burnham (2009), and Leadbeater and Wong (2010), among others, Mike constantly engages in a process of professional formation. He *forms* himself as a principal. He also appreciates that context, era and personal philosophy dictate that there is no single endpoint as a principal—that there is always a need to revisit one's perspectives and practices, to *re-form*. This process of re-formation also requires a high degree of openness, and the capacity and willingness to *de-form* one's leadership practices as one engages in processes of re-formation.

Rather than a negation of previous thinking, this is a process that builds on previous practice and insight, is influenced by new theory and reflection, and leads to a strengthening of his personal philosophy. His leadership philosophy then becomes the basis for an ongoing process of reflection and, importantly, meta-reflection. He describes his guiding philosophy as "eclectic" because it draws on multiple aspects of his experiences:

> Ultimately, the role of any principal is to facilitate the learning of students and staff. The principal is equally a learner. I learn from theory ... I draw on my experiences, and I reflect on my current practice and how it could be improved. I consult the staff about my leadership, and empower them to lead. It is important to ask questions, not least of all about the way in which I reflect. My philosophy depends on making myself vulnerable, questioning the ways in which I reflect, always questioning ... to do this I have to have a firm foundation—and that foundation is my personal philosophy.

With a powerful philosophy to support his leadership actions, Mike believes that he can empower others to lead without being threatening or threatened. He believes that every teacher is a leader: they lead the learning of students and their peers. To be effective leaders, they too need to develop a firm philosophical foundation based on their values, knowledge, understanding, practices and reflections. They too need to be eclectic. They too need to take from many theorists and experiences and apply their learning to specific contexts.

This view challenges professional educators to address the following questions:

- Do you, as a school leader, have a clearly articulated philosophy of leadership and pedagogy?
- To what extent has reflective practice become a slogan rather than a professional practice?
- Does reflection need to be an individual process, or can it be shared usefully?
- To what extent is an individual's professional practice underpinned by values in an explicit way?
- How do practitioners develop and *re-form* their personal philosophies?
- What are the theoretical and practical connections between values, philosophy and professional practice?

These are questions that emerge from Mike's story, that drive his relentless curiosity, and that underline his pervasive philosophy of educational leadership.

Suggested further reading

Fennell, H. (2005). Living leadership in an era of change. *International Journal of Leadership in Education, 8*(2), 145–165.

Friedman, M. S. (2002). *Martin Buber: The life of dialogue* (Vol. 4). New York, NY: Routledge.

Harris, A., & Lambert, L. (2003). *Building leadership capacity for school improvement.* Philadelphia, PA: Open University Press.

Hopkins, D. (2006). *Every school a great school:* London, UK: Specialist Schools and Academies Trust.

Lumby, J., & English, F. (2009). From simplicism to complexity in leadership identity and preparation: Exploring the lineage and dark secrets. *International Journal of Leadership in Education, 12*(2), 95–114.

References

Buber, M. (2002). *Between man and man.* London, UK: Routledge.

Giles, D. L. (2008). *Exploring the teacher–student relationship in teacher education: A hermeneutic phenomenological inquiry.* Unpublished doctoral thesis, Auckland University of Technology. Retrieved from http://hdl.handle.net/10292/537

Leadbeater, C., & Wong, A. (2010). *Learning from extremes.* San Jose, CA: Cisco Systems.

West-Burnham J. (2009). *Rethinking educational leadership.* London, UK: Continuum.

CHAPTER 5

Relational Leadership in a Primary School Setting

Darrell Latham

Richard Newton
Principal, Lee Stream School (1990–1994)
Principal, Halfway Bush School (1994–1999)
Principal, St Clair School (1999–present)

Introduction

Relational leadership is based on the belief that the effectiveness of a principal is contingent upon creating positive organisational relationships that lead to the development of successful learning communities. Respect, integrity, personal regard for others and professional competence are dimensions of relational leadership at the heart of successful schools. St Clair School principal Richard Newton reveals how he facilitates conditions for relational leadership that are central to school improvement and a successful principalship.

Background

St Clair School is a high-performing school located in a beach-side suburb in South Dunedin. The school has a roll of 355 children, and a recent 2010 Education Review Office (ERO) report confirmed that St Clair School has sustained and increased its levels of high performance. In the latest ERO review the school's decile rating has changed from 5 to 6. The school's gender composition is 52 percent boys and

48 percent girls. European/Pākehā children comprise 71 percent of the children, Māori 11 percent, Asian 6 percent and Other 12 percent.

The pupil catchment draws from a socio-economically diverse population, which Richard describes as ranging from homes with fewer resources through to some very wealthy people. This reinforces the school's special character as one that serves two rather different communities. As he explains, "Drawing that together on one site is a wonderful challenge and we put a lot of time into the values, programmes, working effectively together in groups ... and we see that as part of the special character of the school."

Grounded in the day-to-day practicalities of school life, Richard takes this all in his stride. In typical fashion he responded positively to a request to be shadowed by the writer to gather data relating to this case study of principal leadership. While this is not unusual, further discussion suggested that currently life for this principal was anything but normal. St Clair School is in the middle of a major building redevelopment programme and, unbeknown to the writer, in two days' time, ERO personnel would commence a comprehensive review of school programmes.

The last thing any principal would welcome at such a stressful time is a researcher comparing principals' self perceptions of their success with the observer's interpretation of their success strategies. Not in this case: "Feel welcome to come along at 9 am on Monday morning and sit in on our initial meeting," says Richard calmly. He adds that "On Tuesday at 3 pm, teachers meet with ERO to evaluate as a team the effectiveness of school programmes and leadership and you should feel welcome to come along and observe."

It is clear from meeting and talking with Richard that he is the epitome of a successful principal, and that in modelling what successful principals do he brings out the best in his teachers. As a principal he is acutely aware of his role and responsibility as the leader of learning, and he demonstrates his awareness of the research related to effective leadership through his actions. According to Richard, "I think when you do see effective leadership and you see the power and the influence it has in a school and on children, that naturally makes you more inclined to think about doing that yourself." In a typically self-effacing manner he claims no credit for this and praises colleagues that he has worked with as "pivotal in his thinking about leadership."

Richard's overall leadership style could be described as open and effective, with a view to continual improvement

Richard's overall leadership style could be described as open and effective, with a view to continual improvement. Talk leadership with him and do not expect to get ensnared within the educational leadership literature. He is a pragmatist, attuned to school situations, and he has an innate ability to get alongside teachers and children in a positive, supportive and practical way. So, what characteristics and dimensions contribute to making Richard a successful principal and how does he go about bringing out the best in teachers while at the same time exemplifying his own leadership?

Observation suggests that as a principal Richard has a high degree of self-motivation, tends to have a very positive attitude towards his job, and believes that he can make a difference in the lives of learners, teachers and the community. The way Richard works and his relationship with people indicate someone who has a high degree of job satisfaction, who influences people, who is clear about his role, and who has a sense of challenge in his work. He also has a positive perception of the organisation of his school in terms of senior team leadership, organisational structure, the teachers and the school culture.

Influence by expectation and involvement

Richard is positive by nature and always sees the bright side of what might be perceived as challenging situations. Where other principals may have preferred not to have a researcher observe their interaction with ERO, and its potential implications, Richard's attitude was very much focused on active research and allowing the researcher to see the real workings of the school and his principalship. The ERO staff were focused, pleasant and professional, as was Richard. While the three reviewers knew exactly what they wanted, Richard, far from taking a back seat, led the discussion and pre-empted many of the reviewers' questions by having at hand extensive documentation and evidence of his school's compliance in areas of interest. Notwithstanding the fact he was well organised and able in taking the discussion to the ERO staff, Richard also had longitudinal data available, which had been thoroughly analysed, with conclusions drawn in preparation for the next step in the process.

One might conclude from the calmness and sense of assurance conveyed by Richard and his leadership team that this ERO review was a routine visit and of moderate significance. This would be a false impression. Richard displayed a sense of confidence that only comes through knowing his staff, his students and his community. He was well prepared for the review of his school, because prior to "talking the talk" with ERO staff he had "walked the walk" by developing a successful school and principalship.

Richard is often asked to speak to first-time principals and always makes a point of saying to them that they have the best job in the world: "Not the easiest job, but the best job." He feels a real passion when he thinks about the things the job lets him do, the diversity of the work involved, his interest in the work and the challenges he faces.

What became obvious in discussion and when observing Richard is that he perceives, believes and actions his principalship on the basis of making a difference in the lives of those around him. He conveys in his interactions a real sense of "If we do our job well, it will make a difference, not just to the children but to others as well." His communication to staff is clear, consistent and diplomatic, and he models appropriate principal behaviour.

They have the best job in the world: "Not the easiest job, but the best job"

Richard shares in the playground duty—the bane of a busy teacher's working life—and was observed modelling how he expects teachers to interact with the students. Interaction between Richard and his students is obvious, and it is clear that his students respect him and that he cares for them. The way that children sought first aid help, guidance and affirmation could not be construed in any other way than as spontaneous interaction with, and respect for, an affirming school principal.

Richard has high expectations for student achievement and outcomes and is aware that his leadership practices influence learning. His relationships with the teachers and students are interactive and stand out as a feature of the school environment. His influence on student learning outcomes is manifested in the way he promulgates school goals, develops the school structure, and facilitates the growth of social networks, interpersonal relationships and the organisational culture within the school.

As principal, Richard has clarity of purpose and an expectation that his staff will develop a school in which the students are capable socially, emotionally and academically. He clearly articulates his expectation that every child should be the best they can be, whatever that might mean for that child. In Richard's words, it is important that "every child feels connected and valued and that families feel valued. I think that's particularly important in a school." By sanctioning high standards and expectations for children, a similar expectation is conveyed to teachers that they also develop as learners and be the best they can be.

Collaboration, performance and praise

Richard's leadership style reflects the concept of the school as a community of learners, in that collaboration is the norm and teachers regularly review programmes and performance. Teachers are encouraged to experiment and collaborate on matters important to teaching and learning. During this research, after-school staff meetings covered the post-ERO review and discussed future directions for the school. Also evident during these meetings was the extensive collaboration related to the new buildings. Although Richard had certainly thought through the possibilities for the new teaching spaces and how they could best be incorporated into the school, there was no evidence of him promulgating his own ideas about how the physical space would be utilised.

It was clear that Richard had set the scene for staff collaboration, though. He did this by creatively eliciting written or other responses about how the interior space might look, ways they could enhance in-school and community connectedness, and ideas for how the space could be used. A tour of the new building gave all staff the opportunity as a group to view the extension. Staff were encouraged to deliberate in teams and come up with ideas and suggestions, which were further discussed at the staff meeting. Of course, Richard had his own ideas as to how the space could be developed, but no conclusions were drawn and the consultation process was open, genuine and inclusive.

Facilitating connections to families is important to Richard. His openness to parents and teachers is apparent, and is consistent with his aim of acting as a positive role model for everybody in the school and finding time for everyone. My observing Richard in his role aligned with his stated wish to be transparent in the way he works, to ask open-ended questions and to be non-judgemental, so that everyone feels valued and empowered. He believes that anyone can lead if given the right circumstances, and so he looks for opportunities to facilitate leadership in others.

Richard acknowledges that being the principal in a school with 22 teachers means that, although he can touch base with teachers every day or second day and make visits to classrooms, actually making any sort of deeper connection is quite a challenge. This has made him much more aware of his leadership style, and, importantly, means that he now works far more closely in terms of vision and purpose with the school leadership team. He believes that this has made his staff strongly aligned as a group, which was most apparent during the ERO review.

> *He now works far more closely in terms of vision and purpose with the school leadership team*

Richard takes great satisfaction in observing the staff as a cohesive whole and when people in different teams are chatting, socialising, interacting. He believes strongly that if teachers are going to do a good job for children then the teachers need to be united. He also believes that leadership is about being supportive, regularly praising and acknowledging others in their work, and being reflective and considered in decision making. Recognising each member of the school community and their differing needs requires a high level of emotional intelligence and the ability to read people. These traits can be clearly observed in the way he fulfils his role as principal. However, according to Richard, these are skills that are learnt and developed:

> I think the biggest influence was seeing good principalship in the schools that I was in as a scale A teacher, and respecting those people and the work they did and the way they managed themselves, the way they thought about teaching and learning, the way they thought about their relationship with the staff. It gave me a very clear big picture of what school leadership was all about.

Richard clearly articulates the importance of team work and modelling. It is apparent from the way he works with teachers as individuals, and in teams, that he shares power, encourages leadership and develops a climate of trust, collaboration and cooperation, which, in turn, enables him to gain respect and support for his ideas. Encouraging teacher involvement in the early planning stages rather than taking a directive approach ensures buy-in, and again is evidence of Richard's partnership style of leadership.

As an example of how Richard combines his collaborative working style with high expectations, he sees his job as leading with real clarity and being very explicit about what he feels the school needs. He perceives that his leadership role is "not about standing up and beating the drum, but rather working with a team of teachers, where an open invitation is extended to anybody who wants to be involved in a project or practice." As an example, Richard had high expectations for improving literacy at the school and a very clear set of outcomes that he wished to achieve, outcomes that would certainly require a change in teacher practice. He notes that the whole team bought into his proposal and that the implementation of the new literacy programme went extremely well, with a transformation taking place in the way that people taught, assessed and supported the children to develop their writing. Richard also notes that student attainment in writing shifted significantly as a result.

"Connectedness" is a word Richard uses often, and he is clear in his expectation that the professionals in the school also feel connected. He sees connectedness as being particularly important in the workplace, and he wants everyone, "from teachers through to support staff", to feel valued in their work regardless of what they do. He wants his staff to feel that he personally values them, and to feel a sense of connection to the vision of the school so that everybody in the school realises that children matter, that learning is central to what the school does, that learning transcends social, academic and emotional differences, and that families matter. Richard's focus on connectedness reveals a principal who understands the significance of shared leadership, performance and praise. He also perceives connectedness as a professional resource—as a way to facilitate the delivery of consistent value to his students, teachers and the wider communities in which he works.

Leading learning and life in the wider context

For the children, school life is an amalgam of social, emotional and academic needs and differences. Richard has a holistic design for the school, the children, the wider community and the teachers he serves. He sees his vision as creating a school that is *purposeful*: "I quite like that word, and that our purpose is about children developing and growing as people and that encompasses all it means to be a real person." Developing children academically and leading learning is a given for Richard, and he sees these as core functions of what a good school does. However, further discussion reveals that he feels passionately that schools do far more than this, and that the whole idea of the children becoming a competent social community is important to him and something he feels strongly about. Certainly, "quite a lot of what we talk about at school is not about managing children, but helping children to manage themselves."

His personal assessment of success supports his wider aspiration of developing the whole person

His personal assessment of success supports his wider aspiration of developing the whole person. However, in doing so the central focus of leading learning is not compromised. Richard perceives his principalship as having a broad focus on his vision. He aims to remain true to that goal and not to convey any ambiguity in his response, which he says would be quickly identified.

He remains consistent in how he sees things, and one quickly sees that the central focus for him is his overarching advocacy for children. Richard comments that "if a teacher is struggling with a child, I try to be very supportive with them." At the same time, he will uphold the sense of purpose of the school, to which he is strongly committed. From Richard's perspective, every child is worthy, every child is a learner and every child is capable. Again, he sees his role in the widest possible context, not only as a leader of professional learning but also as a very strong role model and mentor for children and teachers.

Richard leads learning via an up-front approach to dealing with everyday matters and responding to curriculum change with his team. However, in the wider school and community context he understands that a direct approach may not always produce the best results. Consistent with his holistic style and the school's focus on "developing capable, caring and confident children who are able to contribute to the community", Richard places an emphasis on making connections with families. However, while always showing openness to parents, he takes care to manage any sense of exasperation he may feel in difficult situations so that this is not conveyed to teachers. He is firmly grounded in the concept of modelling and aims to be a positive role model for everybody in the school. When things are not going well, rather than feeling any sense of injustice or seeking to find fault, he sees this as an opportunity to lead from the front. "I mean, if things are not going well, then that is when there is a real need for leadership."

Sustaining successful leadership

One might assume that Richard regularly faces demanding and challenging situations and resolves them with ease. However, he is candid about striving to maintain a positive profile, the efforts he makes to deal with difficult circumstances, and his perspective on his role as principal. He notes that as he has changed roles in schools and schools have got bigger and more complicated, he has become aware of the need to change his strategies accordingly. As a principal in a smaller school Richard found that it was possible to control things through his enthusiasm for the job and the energy that flowed from this. However, once staffing numbers get above eight teachers, "then things get more complicated." When he first came to St Clair School Richard realised that being the principal of 22 teachers required quite a different approach and strategy. Working with a larger number of people has meant that, as much as he would like to, it is not possible for him to touch base with teachers every day, so working closely with the leadership team has been important.

Richard is candid about how he perceives the challenges of his principalship and how he works to sustain school success. The suggestion that it gets easier with experience and with a management team to deal with pressing issues in a larger school is quickly dismissed in an honest and frank way. Richard sees the principal's role as getting harder, stating "I don't think that it would ever be an easy job and it would only be so if you were dealing with things in a very shallow way."

In order to sustain school success at St Clair School, Richard has instituted a series of ongoing projects. Some of these have been practical projects, such as the building programme, which he describes as not being central to his work, but they have still given him immense satisfaction as "curious distractions", particularly when they are linked to teaching and learning. In this sense, although not directly associated with what he regards as his key role of improving teaching and learning, these secondary projects have indirectly benefited Richard's own thinking about education.

Other challenges include Ministry of Education contracts, such as Extending High Standards across Schools (EHSAS), which he found to be a "fantastic challenge" over four years and which provided another level of interest and dimension to his work. EHSAS is a government initiative designed to raise student achievement by promoting excellence among the country's schools. Highly achieving schools demonstrating good practice have been identified and supported to improve their understanding of the existing processes and practices that are leading to improved student outcomes, or to develop a new idea to enhance their performance.

He also enjoys his involvement in the Principals' Mentors programme. Once again this demonstrates that this principal cares and is keen to share his knowledge and experience with others. At the same time, Richard recognises that the mentors' programme has its own advantages, in that working with young principals gives him access to "the latest knowledge and trends in education." Working with young principals and new principals means gaining new ideas and tackling new challenges: "For me, it is actually a very important part of what I do." Although the responsibility of being part of the programme is clearly draining, the payoff is that he finds it professionally invigorating.

Overall, Richard is happy to remain in the same school and in the same job. He is sustained by the fact that his principal's role is never quite the same. It is constantly evolving and changing, and he clearly relishes the challenge.

Conclusion

The position of principal in any school is framed around leadership and influence. The effectiveness of any principal's leadership, and their degree of influence, depends on numerous factors, particularly how the incumbent perceives their role. Richard's commitment to his role as principal of St Clair School is evident in his personal and professional approach. He conveys high expectations of teachers and students alike. He supports his teachers and actively involves them in the decision-making process, while allowing them the autonomy to be creative. He leads learning, judiciously invokes the power of authority, and models effective leadership practice.

Richard Newton is an exemplary principal, who displays warmth, empathy and reliability. He lacks pretentiousness and is alert to human subtleties. He aims to bring out the best in the students, teachers and the community in which he serves.

Reflections for readers

Developing relational leadership in schools is about building people through day-to-day social exchanges and actions. These exchanges and actions lead to the development of conditions that are more likely to facilitate student achievement and school improvement. In an influential study, Bryk and Schneider (2002) found that social exchanges and the development of trust are key components in bringing about progress and change in a school. Their research draws on longitudinal data gathered from principals, teachers, parents and community leaders, and reveals that effective social relationships and, in particular, the development of relational trust, aids school improvement. In this case, relational trust can be defined as "the interpersonal exchanges that take place in a school community; principal to teacher, principal to parent, teacher to teacher, teacher to student, and teacher to parent" (Bryk & Schneider, 2002, p. 1), and is at the heart of successful school development.

Bryk and Schneider note that the development of relational trust is built on daily social exchanges, supporting teachers and facilitating experimentation with new practices. Relational trust cultivates the conditions that encourage individuals to initiate and maintain the kinds of activities necessary to influence school improvement. Trust, therefore, can be seen as the glue that holds improving schools together.

In line with Bryk and Schneider's findings, Richard's leadership style incorporates a focus on the dynamics of relationships between teachers, students, parents and the wider community. He has adapted his leadership style in a larger school environment to make greater use of leadership teams and technology, and so relational leadership has not been compromised. These changes are consistent with the research findings of Bryk and Schneider, who found that schools with high relational trust are more likely to work together and experiment with new practices.

Similarly, Tshannen-Moran and Hoy (1998) undertook a review of the literature on trust in schools and concluded that five key components were commonly used to gauge trustworthiness: benevolence, reliability, competence, honesty and openness. In his dealings with teachers, students and the community, Richard demonstrates benevolence by having the best interests of the school at heart. Reliability, as evidenced by acting consistently and fairly, is seen in his ability to perform the tasks required of a principal. Honesty and openness are defined by his integrity and authenticity, the manner in which he represents situations to ERO, staff and students, and the way in which he shares information.

The attributes of successful school leaders are diverse, however. Critical elements include collaboration, building networks and learning communities, and growing the capabilities of others. Successful school leadership is complex and is not a prescribed or mechanical process. It is built on a foundation of trust and integrity and requires leaders who create webs of inclusion, who listen and who are reflective practitioners.

Relational leadership recognises that schools are organisations that meet the needs of a diverse range of people. The framework for emotional literacy posed by Haddon, Goodman, Park and Deakin Crick (2005) places relational leadership at the centre. Authentic leadership encourages that, as part of the reflective process, we should ask ourselves the following questions:

- As a relational leader, am I building character, connectedness, purpose, relationships and a sense of community?
- Do I communicate with all stakeholders and am I future-oriented?
- How do we build and celebrate success in the workplace?

Suggested further reading

Barth, R. S. (2001). *Learning by heart.* San Francisco, CA: Jossey-Bass.

Dressler, L. (2006). *Consensus through conversation: How to achieve high-commitment decisions.* San Francisco, CA: Berrett-Koehler.

DuFour, R., & Eaker, R. (1998). *Professional learning communities at work: Best practices for enhancing student achievement.* Bloomington, IN: National Educational Service.

Eichler, M. (2007). *Consensus organizing: Building communities of mutual self-interest.* Thousand Oaks, CA: Sage.

Eller, J. (2004). *Effective group facilitation in education: How to energize meetings and manage difficult groups.* Thousand Oaks, CA: Corwin Press.

Hoy, W. K., & Tschannen-Moran, M. (2003). The conceptualization and measurement of faculty trust in schools. In W. K. Hoy & C. Miskel (Eds.), *Studies in leading and organizing schools* (pp. 181–207). Greenwich, CT: Information Age.

Kochanek, J. R. (2005). *Building trust for better schools: Research-based practices.* Thousand Oaks, CA: Corwin Press.

Robinson, V. H. J., & Lai, M. K. (2006). *Practitioners research for educators: A guide to improving classrooms and schools.* Thousand Oaks, CA: Corwin Press.

Tye, B. B. (2000). *Hard truths: Uncovering the deep structures of schooling.* New York, NY: Teachers College Press.

References

Bryk, A. S., & Schneider, B. (2002). *Trust in schools: A core resource for improvement.* New York, NY: Russell Sage Foundation.

Haddon, A. Goodman, H. Park, J. & Deakin Crick, R. (2005). Evaluating emotional literacy in schools: The development of the School Emotional Environment for Learning survey, *Pastoral Care in Education, 23*(3), 4–16.

Tschannen-Moran, M., & Hoy, W. K. (1998). Trust in schools: A conceptual and empirical analysis. *Journal of Educational Administration, 36*(3/4), 334–352.

CHAPTER 6

Leadership Focused on an Ethic of Care

Alaster Gibson

Richard Inder
Principal, Otamarakau School (1992–1994)
Principal, Pongakawa School (1995–1999)
Principal, Gate Pa School (2000–present)

Introduction

Richard Inder is an inspiring educational leader who is passionate about teaching and learning, a principal who believes in modelling a values-based, relational style of leadership. The story told in this chapter focuses on Richard's leadership in turning around, rebranding and rebuilding a failing primary school and transforming it into a caring, innovative, learning-focused community. It is a story of crafted wisdom and indomitable positivity.

Background

Richard loved teaching from the outset. Following his first teaching position in Christchurch, he moved north to the Bay of Plenty with his wife, where he gained invaluable experience teaching at the Opotiki, Te Teko and Kawarau South schools. He taught at Kawarau South for 5 years before moving into the role of senior teacher. Then, after serving as deputy principal for 18 months, Richard realised that he was now ready to be principal.

Richard's work in rural schools led to his being offered a teaching principal's position at a small three-teacher school in the rural settlement of Otamarakau. This was around the time of Tomorrow's Schools and the move towards the current decentralised system of school governance based on boards of trustees. A few years later Richard and his family moved to another rural settlement, Pongakawa, where Richard enjoyed a further 5 formative years as the principal of the local primary school. During this time at Pongakawa he became aware of the problems at the nearby Tauranga South Primary School, as it was then known. The school's board of trustees had resigned, two successive commissioners had been appointed and the student roll was in decline. Following the resignation of the incumbent principal in 1999, Richard applied for, and secured, the position of principal at Tauranga South School, beginning in 2000. Reflecting back on that period Richard says:

> I had many comments as to why on earth I would apply for that position, and leave the idyllic Pongakawa setting. I suppose my attitude was that it might be the ultimate challenge as a great opportunity of turning things around.

Gate Pa School

Soon after taking up the principalship at Tauranga South, Richard set about rebranding the school in consultation with the local community. The name Gate Pa School was chosen to acknowledge the historical and bicultural roots of the local community. The school caters for approximately 350 children, and a special aspect of this decile 2 school community is its cultural diversity, comprising approximately 50 percent Māori, 25 percent Pākehā/European and 25 percent children from other cultural backgrounds. The school's motto is "We care."

Richard describes the children at Gate Pa School as very appreciative and affectionate, adding that "In this school you get lots of hugs and lots of hugs are fine, it is a stand-out feature of the school." He also regards the children as resilient in spite of the difficulties they have to deal with. Richard believes that every parent has a talent, and he encourages parents to get to know the staff and to contribute to the life of the school community. The priorities in Richard's leadership strategy are to model positive relationships and to seek to build strong relationships between teachers, students and parents/caregivers.

The priorities in Richard's leadership strategy are to model positive relationships and to seek to build strong relationships between teachers, students and parents/caregivers

Challenges

Richard describes his job as "very much a juggling act, as you make your time available for the children, for the teachers, for the parents and also for the wider community and the wider profession." Richard believes that parents want the best for their children but that sometimes, they struggle to know how to do that. He contends that although staff are not trained to be social workers, the reality is they often have to address a range of social issues as they educate the children. The recent economic recession has put extra pressure on family relationships and finances, especially among sole-parent and single-income families, many of whom rely on rental accommodation.

Richard describes his job as "very much a juggling act, as you make your time available for the children, for the teachers, for the parents and also for the wider community and the wider profession"

Another challenge the school has to work with is the unpredictable and significant number of transient students (at least a third of the school) who, for various reasons, are enrolled for a brief time and then move on within a given year. A user-pays van is provided to transport students who have relocated to another suburb and whose parents want their children to have continuity and stability of schooling by staying at Gate Pa School. The wide-ranging academic and behavioural needs of the children are seen by Richard as a reflection of wider social issues facing the community:

> I think the needs and behavioural challenges of our school are certainly very intense and we have many children that I suppose live in two worlds, the world at school and the world at home ... It's been heartening for us to just remember the world at school is the world we can control. We can influence the other world at home but we can't control it.

One leadership strategy in response to these challenges has been to try to "get behind the reasons for the behaviour." This can be particularly difficult because teachers often experience issues for which they have had no training. Removing behaviourally disruptive children from the school is not a preferred option: "We have to look very carefully at how we can do our very best supporting the children, and ethically be able to say, well actually, we gave it our best shot." Consistent with his personal, values-based perspective on spirituality, Richard views challenges as opportunities to transform a child's life and to make a difference for the future. These opportunities can be very rewarding, in Richard's opinion, but also very challenging because the issues are so complex: "You have got to use the creative thinking of the whole staff to try and turn around a child's life and that is the specialness about working in this place—is that making a difference is why we are on this staff."

Another strategy for ameliorating behavioural problems has been to create what Richard describes as "the Gate Pa School world", a world that is consistently based on the school ethic of care. Richard intentionally seeks to create a positive organisational culture, one that portrays a world that is exciting for the students and holds a future for them. The social climate of the Gate Pa School world needs to be different to the negativity found in the media and in some of the local neighbourhoods. Mondays can be challenging, because the children arrive back from the weekend in their "other world." The staff view Monday as a day to settle the children back into their learning. Richard also mentions the importance of humour. When asked if Gate Pa School is a happy place, Richard responds positively, adding, "We have got a happy staff, they enjoy each other's company, they work hard, they are very professional, we have a lot of laughs, but we have some tough days in the office as well."

Richard believes that low-decile schools require a "special breed of teachers" with a wide range of interpersonal skills in managing children, showing empathy and building relationships with children and parents. Recruiting the right sort of teacher to work at Gate Pa School is therefore a leadership role that Richard is intent on doing well: "If a vacancy becomes available, and they are all crucial, from caretakers to teachers' aides, then if I get the right person for that particular job and grow them, it makes my job much easier." Richard explains that the children are able to "read you like a radar" because of the challenging life experiences they have had to endure, especially those involving relationships with adults who have let them down. He emphasises the importance of being genuine and serving from the heart:

> They can look us in the eye and they can scan us very easily and they can tell if we are genuine, that we care, that we are professional about our job. We should never under-estimate a little five-year-old being able to do that.

Leadership philosophy

Richard has crafted his leadership style over many years of professional experience:

> I think you get wiser in this job ... I am becoming more critical of my time, what I should be doing, and why am I being asked to do these other things that aren't to do with teaching and learning.

In explaining his views, Richard cites the best evidence synthesis of research on school leadership (Robinson, Hohepa, and Lloyd, 2009), which he believes provides clear support for principals to prioritise leadership in teaching and learning.

Richard's thinking has been influenced by positive and negative experiences of the educational leaders he has worked with. He is also actively involved in the Western Bay of Plenty Principals' Association and has a strong network of principal colleagues with whom he can discuss professional matters: "They model to me, and it's very important."

Richard describes the leadership of the school as having become very "horizontal" and widely distributed across a staff comprising two associate principals, 15 full-time and two part-time teachers. The associate principals and the principal work as a leadership team, whose focus is mostly future-oriented. A management team comprising syndicate team leaders and the principal take care of the day-to-day operation. Richard describes his job as keeping "the bus going in the right direction." Other forms of distributed leadership include staff taking lead roles in various sports and curriculum areas.

One of Richard's key philosophies is to protect staff from unnecessary administrative distractions and to provide them with as much support as possible, especially in relation to challenging behaviours and ensuring they are able to provide effective teaching and learning programmes. He believes *The New Zealand Curriculum* (Ministry of Education, 2007) provides "a wonderful opportunity for creativity in developing a Gate Pa School curriculum with a lot of freedom to pursue what's appropriate for teaching our kids."

In his experience, Richard believes that the principal's leadership role has become more complex over the years and he hopes this will change. Compared to principals he has met overseas, those in New Zealand have to contend with a much wider range of responsibilities: "There are far too many things that I have to do, from finances ... property is a huge one, and the very nature of being a principal in a New Zealand school." Richard does not believe principals should be property project managers. However, he is passionate about protecting his time with students and teachers in classrooms. His approach is to "delegate the stuff you don't need to be doing that other people can do and get out into the classroom ... you get a feel for what's happening in your school." He still finds it difficult to maintain the time he would like to spend with children and teachers.

You have got to say to yourself, "I am going to put aside some money for my development because it's in the best interest for everybody, you just have to get that global perspective"

Staying on top of the game is also important to Richard. One way he achieves this is by keeping in touch with developments in education in New Zealand and overseas by attending national and international conferences. In 2009 he attended a 5-day conference in Kuala

Lumpur, where he found the quality time for discussions with other principals was invaluable: "You have got to say to yourself, I am going to put aside some money for my professional development because it's in the best interest for everybody, you just have to get that global perspective."

Another successful leadership strategy Richard models is maintaining a healthy work–life balance. Although he clearly enjoys his job, the professional demands are such that he emphasises to the staff the importance of taking holiday breaks and spending time away from school work:

> The job is unique in that you are dealing with people's lives. You know you can and have got to make a difference with the situations that you face every day. It is a challenge emotionally, it is draining. So I and the staff enjoy our time away from teaching and that's important.

Key accomplishments

When Richard took up the role of principal at Tauranga South Primary (now Gate Pa School), the staff were "emotionally fragile." He held a series of meetings in which the staff were invited to engage in a self-review process. To help Richard gain some ideas for the path ahead, the staff were asked to identify what they felt needed to change and what was important to retain. During the first of these meetings he remembers one teacher saying that when she attended a professional development day prior to 2000 she had felt ashamed to identify herself as a teacher from Tauranga South School. Richard said, "That sort of stuck with me for a long time as something that we have to change."

This negative morale was turned around not as the result of any "one significant change, just lots and lots of little steps." One of these little steps included changing the school name, to start with a fresh identity that connected strongly with the wider community and the early Māori and European history of the area. Other steps involved bringing on board the right sort of staff when vacancies became available. Introducing a strong values system into the school also played a part in moving the school out of its troubled past. As Richard says, "They [the staff] valued values, but they probably didn't have them articulated in a way that they had them all on board."

This negative morale was turned around not as the result of any "one significant change, just lots and lots of little steps"

Richard also tells of consistently looking for authentic ways of improving the school to build a positive reputation in the local community. He feels it is important to have an attractive, rubbish- and graffiti-free, well-maintained school environment for the students. Visitors to the school are impressed by its attractive physical environment, believing that it looks like a decile 10 school. Richard says this pride in the school environment permeates down to the way students talk, the way they wear their uniforms and the way they treat others.

A vivid example of where Richard was able to make a tangible difference in people's lives involved a behaviourally disturbed student who was close to being suspended. Richard and the chairperson of the school board of trustees met with the boy's mother and honestly expressed their concerns, without judgment, in the hope of finding a collective and supportive solution to the problem. The mother took on board the concerns raised and it was decided she would come to the school with her child from 9 am to 3 pm. She also has morning tea in the staffroom, which has enabled her to build a positive relationship with the staff. Although the child still needs his mother to mind him during the day, Richard believes that the boy looks happier and healthier: "Mum probably didn't have a very good knowledge of the school and now she does, and she sees teachers in a different light … and that has turned this child around." As Richard points out, it can be very hard to appreciate sometimes how difficult it is for a single mother who has come through a background of drug and alcohol abuse, domestic violence, split marriage/partners, rental housing, benefits and struggling to makes ends meet. He summarises this episode as follows:

> It's very rewarding when you see you have managed to solve something that was very hard to solve. You can't pick up any books to say well, OK, this is what you do, this is the recipe for this problem. You have to be creative and resourceful … we have had some good successes.

Vision for Gate Pa School

Richard's vision for Gate Pa is for the school to become a model for low-decile schools across New Zealand. The school has a good reputation in Tauranga, runs quality programmes with quality staff and, as Richard puts it, "can make that difference." Already children are coming to Gate Pa from other areas and a number of international students have enrolled. To realise his vision for the school, Richard intends to utilise the "magic" of the new New Zealand curriculum and to develop a curriculum that is appropriate for the students at Gate Pa:

> We have a themed approach each term … in term one it was kai moana [food from the sea], a science-based unit … taking students to local surroundings, taking kids fishing, taking their families. It's very well attended as far as parental involvement goes. It's good, rich teaching and learning.

His vision is to consistently provide the same rich educational experience for all students, each term of the school year, and to continually look for ways to enhance children's learning. That, for Richard, is the next important step: to have that richness, and children waking up in the morning, dying to get to school, talking about their learning. Richard believes that the integrity and the quality of teaching and learning, and students' love of school, are the best marketing tools a school can have.

> *To have that richness, and children waking up in the morning, dying to get to school*

One obstacle to this vision is information and communication technology (ICT), because of the costs involved for financially pressured families. On the other hand, although Richard continues to try to provide access to good-quality educational ICT, he also has a feeling that it is over-rated. He believes strongly that "these kids need people first and they need those relationships and those connections we get through face to face, through people—and ICT should only be a tool to enhance that." In reflecting on his arrival at Tauranga South School, Richard says that the school had invested a lot of money in a computer suite and it had crippled them financially. His vision for the school is, therefore, to balance the need for ICT with what is affordable, and to ensure that the most important things—quality teachers and teaching—are maintained for all students.

Leadership initiatives

Richard recalls that in 2003 there was an interesting group of boys in the junior part of the school. At the time he realised he would need to make some proactive leadership decisions to help them achieve success in their education, because "life's going to be pretty tough unless *we* change something." His willingness to explore new initiatives, together with his concern with the way Gate Pa would cater for boys, led to the idea of introducing boys-only classes. The school engaged in research and professional development on the topic of boys' education and enlisted a teacher who was passionate about getting the initiative up and running. The classes are specially designed to cater for the needs of active boys who need a different approach to teaching and learning. Richard found that the initiative with boys-only classes also had positive learning effects on mixed classes.

In the past 2 years Richard has identified a similar need emerging among the girls in the school. He sees providing for girls who are at risk as the next real issue facing primary and intermediate schools in New Zealand. Whereas the focus on boys' learning was primarily to address their underachievement in literacy, Richard perceives a growing need to address social issues with girls. Accordingly, Gate Pa

School now provides a girls-only camp programme where "We teach them some girls stuff, relationships, and fashion." They have also started a girls' club, which meets during lunch break.

The school has also been utilising Ministry of Education funding and resources to build more effective relationships with its Pasifika families. They have run several forums on literacy and the school's educational philosophy for Pasifika parents. Richard has become aware of the importance of building relationships with Pasifika families before they arrive at the school and believes this work can be done in the home or in the preschool prior to five. The aim of this initiative is to help all children—not just Pasifika children—to successfully transition into the school learning environment.

Richard attributes the success in turning the school around to the collective input from everyone in the organisation. He says he is very blessed in having staff who work hard and are very professional:

> They laugh, they cry and don't shy away, they take on board new things, they are willing to give things a go and often we hear good ideas and we say OK, let's try it and give it a go and they do ... they are open to exploring in creative ways.

For Richard, the "unsung heroes" are the support staff:

> We have absolutely amazing support staff ... they are not highly paid yet they go the extra mile ... they do a very important job and they go far beyond the call of duty ... there's not enough of them ... they all have their skills and areas within the team.

Resilience in leadership

Richard attributes his sustained leadership to a range of factors. First and foremost, he acknowledges and honours his wife, Chris, whom he describes as an excellent teacher, wife and mother. Richard values his family life. He and Chris have three children, who are talented and successful in a variety of ways, "so they have kept us real." He also values his space away from school, which is always demanding of his time. He does value his privacy, so "most of our weekends are just chilling out."

Richard enjoys physical exercise such as a walk along the beach, playing tennis and going fishing. He also has a wide circle of non-teaching friends, such as farmers and kiwifruit growers, and he enjoys their company because he can't "talk shop." Richard works to maintain a healthy work–life balance, which is something he acknowledges he had to learn through experience. As a rural school principal he was provided with a school house. While of some financial benefit, the house was also something of a trap, because it made it very easy to return to school during week nights and in the weekends. Having learnt from these experiences, Richard now says:

> I have adopted the philosophy, well if it's not finished or done by 5 o'clock on a Friday, it can wait. It's all very well me saying that but that's after a few years of experience as a principal. I try not to take a lot of work home.

Conclusion

Richard Inder's principal leadership at Gate Pa School is inspiring because of who he is, the caring values that he models, his passion for teaching and learning, and the 10 years' sustained commitment he has given to his staff, students and the wider parent community. Richard's story is about crafted wisdom learned through experience. It reflects his humility and professional courage in stepping out of the comfort zone, working hard and collaboratively to turn around a troubled, low-decile school. Listening to him, one cannot help but pick up his passion, perseverance and purpose—to make a difference in people's lives and to provide hope for the future. His story is a tribute to an effective New Zealand educational leader who has integrity and credibility, a man who loves his family, is other-focused, and who recognises the importance of a healthy work–life balance.

Reflections for readers

Richard's story demonstrates the complexity of educational leadership. It also highlights the challenge of leading the transformation of a failing school. This relates to an important dual role school principals fill, which is to "Manage the day-to-day operation of the school *and* lead the development of improved teacher performance and education" (Education Review Office, 1996, p. 5). Within the daily leadership and management of a modern school there is a constant underlying theme of how principals manage the change process, particularly in relation to leading a professional community of learners. In discussing leading through change, Fullan (2001, p. 44) suggests

> It is a particular kind of re-culturing for which we strive: one that activates and deepens moral purpose through collaborative work cultures that respect differences and constantly build and test knowledge against measurable results—a culture within which one realizes that sometimes being off balance is a learning moment.

Readers might therefore reflect on their own institutional contexts and ask why change might be needed, and what change might be necessary and desirable:
- How might I encourage the development of appropriate attitudes, skills, and processes through which effective change could be achieved and sustained within

the culture of your organisation? Some of you may already be experiencing change within your organisations and be able to reflect on how well this change is being articulated and achieved, and how it might be improved.

Richard's leadership story also emphasises the importance of modelling an ethic of care in leadership practice. This relates to a wide body of literature that emphasises values and interpersonal relationships in effective leadership practice; for example, ethical and virtuous leadership (Lashway, 1996), authentic leadership (Cashman, 1998) and relational leadership (Dyer, 2011). Recent qualitative research into spirituality in principal leadership (Gibson, 2011) found that principals' personal and professional integrity, their quality care of staff, coupled with professional competence were perceived to be influential by teacher participants. Fullan (2001, p. 51) argues, "If moral purpose is job one, relationships are job two, as you can't get anywhere without them."

- How important is the modelling of values such as caring relationships and maintaining integrity within leadership practice?

In a similar vein, readers might like to reflect on further questions arising from this case study:

- Positivity through leadership has a major impact on the lives of students, teachers and parents/caregivers. How might levels of positivity be enhanced in the life of your community?
- Consider the degree to which leadership is genuinely distributed within your educational organisation and how leadership is mentored and managed. What challenges are there in developing leadership capacity in your workplace?
- Take time to reflect on your present levels of resilience. How do you monitor your own well-being? How do you build in personal development for yourself so that you remain refreshed and inspired?

Suggested further reading

Du Four, R. (2002). The learning-centred principal. *Educational Leadership*, 59(8), 12–15.

Noddings, N. (2002). *Educating moral people: A caring alternative to character education.* Williston, VT: Teachers College Press.

Razik, T., & Swanson, A. (2001). *Fundamental concepts of educational leadership and management* (2nd ed.). Upper Saddle River, NJ: Prentice Hall.

Sergiovanni, T. (2000). *The lifeworld of leadership: Creating culture, community, and personal meaning in our schools.* San Francisco, CA: Jossey-Bass.

References

Cashman, K. (1998). *Leadership from the inside out*. Provo, UT: Executive Excellence Publishing.

Dyer, K. M. (2001). Relational leadership. *The School Administrator, 58*(10), 28–31.

Education Review Office. (1996). *Professional leadership in primary schools*. Number 7, Winter. Retrieved from http://www.ero.govt.nz/ Publications/eers1996/96no7hl.htm.

Fullan, M. (2001) *Leading in a culture of change*. San Francisco, CA: Jossey-Bass.

Gibson, A. (2011) *Spirituality in principal leadership and its influence on teachers and teaching*. Unpublished doctoral thesis, University of Waikato. Retrieved from http://researchcommons.waikato.ac.nz/bitstream/10289/5176/3/thesis.pdf.

Lashway, L. (1996). Ethical leadership. In S. Smith and P. Piele, (Eds.), *School leadership. Handbook for excellence* (pp. 103–130). Eugene, OR: University of Oregon. (ERIC Clearinghouse on Educational Management.)

Ministry of Education. (2007). *The New Zealand curriculum*. Wellington: Learning Media.

Robinson, V., Hohepa, M., & Lloyd, C. (2009). *School leadership and student outcomes: Identifying what works and why: Best evidence synthesis iteration*. Wellington: Ministry of Education. Retrieved from http://www.educationcounts.govt.nz/publications/series/2515/60169/60170.

CHAPTER 7

Collaborative Leadership in a Specialist School

Lynn Tozer

Jann Carvell
Principal, Fairhaven School (2000–present)

Introduction

Jann Carvell, principal of Fairhaven School in Napier, is passionate about her school. She is a person who encourages growth of the individual and she inspires those with whom she works. She feels that by distributing leadership she will ensure the school as a whole will be sustainable into the future and will be in a position to continue strongly without her. Her drive to build a strong family culture in her school, to build the professional capacity of her staff and to empower her students will be evident in Jann's story.

Principal career pathway

What was the professional journey that led to Jann becoming the leader of this specialist school, which caters for students with a variety of special needs? When her children had reached school age, Jann joined her principal husband at Tirohanga, a two-teacher country school near Taupo, where she taught 5-9 year olds. Although they were very much members of the local school community, this time saw the development of country school clusters, whereby smaller rural schools supported each other and collaborated in inter-school and combined community events. It is interesting to note the impact these early years had on Jann. Today, the theme of "We are family" underpins the Fairhaven School culture and Jann continues to lead a dynamic cluster of special schools.

From Tirohanga, Jann moved to Wairakei School, where she was the junior class teacher. During this time she completed her reading recovery training. This proved to be a valuable qualification when, in 1984, she travelled alone to England. She worked as a nursery teacher of 3-5 year olds at St Luke's, where her role was focused on developing an effective transition-to-school process. This understanding of the importance of the transition points in the lives of her students has continued to underpin her pedagogy within special education.

Jann spent 8 years in her subsequent appointment to Bodmin Infants in Cornwall. This was her first formal role in teaching special needs students. She became a local reading recovery expert and was asked to lecture in reading recovery as a part of the special needs programme at the University College of St Mark and St John. While still working full-time at Bodmin, she travelled throughout Cornwall as an advisor, talking to teachers about the reading recovery programme and its potential benefits. Jann's time at Bodmin Infants mainly focused on the assessment of 2-7 year olds who had been identified as having special needs and for whom a future in mainstream education was being considered.

In 1996 Jann returned to New Zealand. She was appointed as an advisor to work with local referrals to Napier Special Education Services. Initially, the collaborative ethos of the special education team provided a successful working environment, in two special schools particularly. When Jann left the service she was appointed regional coordinator of the Resource Teachers: Learning and Behaviour (RTLB) services in Napier.

Several themes emerged for Jann from these foundational experiences in education: the fundamental importance of family and whānau groupings; the benefits of collaboration when schools cluster; the experience of working with a student with autism, then more broadly in special education; the clear imperative to ensure that the transition points in a student's school life are seamless and successful. It was therefore not surprising that Jann applied for, and secured, the position of principal of Fairhaven School in 2000. As she said, "It was time to implement all of the things that I knew and believed."

Reasons for choosing a leadership role

Jann became a principal because she wanted to make a difference. Having come to special education later in her career, she appreciated that all students are learners and that the children she met in a special education context had so much potential to "unpack." Although Jann had worked in special education in advisory roles, this had not provided the deep fulfilment and satisfaction she sought: "We are not just about *caring*. We are about *education*. [Back then] the disability got in the way and people had such low expectations. Kids with special needs were not being treated as learners." She could see that a principalship would allow her to provide a "wrap-around" service, where she could be instrumental in creating and drawing together elements of a rich, nurturing learning environment for students within special education. As a teacher, Jann had the opportunity to work with these students; but as a principal, with control over finances and decision making, she could initiate her innovative plans and the many ideas others had brought to her. As a principal it was exciting to be able to take on initiatives and to make them work: "It's that *you* decide that it is time to do something and here is a place you can."

Jann became a principal because she wanted to make a difference

Clearly Jann could not do this alone. It was only by having a fully supportive board that this could happen. Fairhaven School has had the same board of trustees for 9 years. As Jann reflects on this she is very clear about the importance of the trusting, open and respectful relationship they have built and maintained: "There is mutual valuing of opinions and ideas, and the school and the board have a truly collaborative vision of the service and culture it is their combined job to create." Jann values highly the expertise and experience in business, in life and in working with a family member with a disability that board members bring to the school. Many answers to the challenges she faces come from board members, and she fully recognises just how much she has to learn from them.

Jann and her board have a "birth to death" vision for their school, in which lifelong learning is a reality and transitions are carefully and seamlessly managed so that students can continue to be supported after they turn 21 years of age. When decisions are made, the resulting actions must be fully and promptly accomplished, with set goals and milestones that are met and evaluated. Jann believes that by making things happen she is fulfilling the board's expectations, is constantly focused on and committed to dynamic school improvement and, above all, is making a real difference for the students.

School and collaborative leadership

When Jann came to Fairhaven in 2000 there were 27 students and the school was under threat of closure. Following the disestablishment of the secondary school units in 1989, Fairhaven had become a small primary-based school which, although autonomous, was strongly influenced by the local schools. However, the Special Education 2000 policy framework, combined with Jann's visionary leadership, enabled Fairhaven to negotiate with a local intermediate school for another classroom and for the re-establishment of a secondary school satellite unit.

Today Fairhaven is a specialist school and resource centre that caters for students between the ages of 5 and 21 with a variety of special needs, intellectual and/or related disabilities, and autistic spectrum disorders. The school has 76 students from nine ethnic groups, 19 teaching staff, 25 teacher aides, five specialist teachers and four ancillary staff. The students can attend either the base school or one of the 11 satellite classes situated in primary, intermediate and secondary schools throughout the greater Napier area. Jann is also proud of the satellite class that has been established at Bridge Pa, which caters for students transitioning into the workforce. This is a joint initiative between Fairhaven and Intellectual Disability Empowerment in Action (IDEA) services.

As an accredited fund holder for students eligible for the Ongoing and Reviewable Resourcing Scheme (ORRS), Fairhaven employs a wide range of specialist staff who bring expertise in music, dance, art, speech and language, physiotherapy, recreational therapy, occupational therapy and behaviour management. The school provides specialist help, extra teaching, teacher aides or equipment as needs are identified, since the funding flexibility allows resources to be used responsively to best meet the needs of individual students. However, as Jann points out:

> Managing this requires vigilance and creativity with staffing. Because children are ORRS funded, with a 0.1 or 0.2 teaching entitlement, if a child leaves or dies, the teaching entitlement goes immediately and so too the teacher-aide position.

Jann has created a staff culture in a fully collaborative and holistic way, ensuring that the highly varied needs, aptitudes and interests of students are catered for. Staff ensure that students are provided with a wide range of education outside the classroom opportunities, including riding for the disabled, swimming and canoeing. Regular visits to places of interest, such as a farm, provide meaningful contexts in which students can practise and transfer learning skills while simply enjoying the experience.

Fairhaven School subscribes to the Award Scheme Development and Accreditation Network (ASDAN), the levels of which provide a structure for meaningful and contextual learning for their secondary students that allows them access to appropriate work opportunities. The aim of ASDAN programmes is to enable young people to understand themselves and others better, and to become prepared for making the transition to adult life. Jann works to ensure that collaboration between staff and the community is ongoing and that senior students participate in workplace and business projects. Inclusion of students as members of New Zealand society is given priority by staff and, where appropriate, students are encouraged and supported to gain external qualifications such as the National Certificate in Employment Skills (NCES) and National Certificate of Educational Achievement (NCEA).

Teachers respond to individual student needs by closely analysing high-quality assessment information, from which individual learning plans identifying learning and skill development in each curriculum area are developed. The personalised learning plans provide detailed information to both inform teaching and ensure effective monitoring of progress. Photographs and stories in individual student portfolios show their progress in learning and social development across a range of learning situations. Teachers and students are further developing their ICT skills to create interactive electronic portfolios, which can be accessed readily by parents and families for appreciation, progress evidence and comment. Jann adds:

> To complement our current appraisal systems, we have also developed teacher e-portfolios which include teachers' philosophy and reflections. Of course, mine is out there too for the staff to read.

High expectations are set and achievements celebrated within the nurturing school culture, underpinned by the "We are family" motto. The school works closely with the wider school community and with other education, community and health services, fulfilling an advocacy role for the students and their families. The inclusive family ethos extends to all those who work with Fairhaven students and their families: "We *are* a family. You can feel it when you walk into the school, and the kids are very caring and supportive of each other."

High expectations are set and achievements celebrated within the nurturing school culture, underpinned by the "We are family" motto

Jann's motivation as a principal is to make a difference by actively making changes to benefit students and their families. Jann leads strongly and gives high priority to ongoing professional learning and development for all staff. The school's well-organised approach to teaching, use of high-quality student achievement data to inform staff professional learning, a generous budget allocation, a system of self-review of current best practice, and a constructive and respectful relationship between trustees, management and staff are all factors that contribute to very positive student outcomes.

Successful leadership strategies

It is evident that, for Jann, principalship is a subtle combination of strong leadership and effective delegation. Creating a thriving, cohesive school "family" culture has required steep learning, profound reflection, much professional research and reading, and some very difficult decisions, including staffing matters. Jann's initial response to becoming a principal was that she had achieved some status and had reached the top. However, this was very quickly followed by the realisation that, along with influence and power, the role carries a great deal of responsibility. Jann saw that her leadership behaviours were an indication of the well-being of the school. She also learned that it was not possible to please everyone.

Creating a thriving, cohesive school "family" culture has required steep learning, profound reflection, much professional research and reading, and some very difficult decisions, including staffing matters

Jann's first strategy was to expand the school, in terms of student numbers and dedicated, qualified staff. When she arrived in 2000 the school was small and in disarray, and it had an ageing staff who were comfortable in their practice. Because the satellite classrooms were at some distance from the base school, there was little positive school culture. Jann's initial attempts to put in place incentives to change staff practice were unsuccessful. She had read much about school culture and knew that deep change was needed. She worked to grow the school roll by catering for, and retaining, students beyond the age of 14 and by actively marketing the school's strengths:

> We had a struggling school and now we have a very successful one. Deep changes were needed at all levels: management, health and safety, governance ... the systems that are in place now are sustainable. Staff say, 'We look like a normal school.' 'Seeing ourselves in positive mirrors' as Cathy Wylie says.

Roll growth led to staff growth and to the deeper change that Jann sought. Careful and deliberate staff selection further moved the school forward. When confronted with change, some staff were pushed beyond their comfort zone and chose to leave. In their place, an innovative, risk-taking and diverse team were chosen, based on their qualifications (all now have degrees) and for the strengths they could bring to the school. Jann and the board of trustees sought staff who were willing to continue to learn and change. They also developed a staff appointment policy that included a professional code of conduct to safeguard all staff, stated expectations of full participation in professional learning, and a requirement to teach anywhere within the school. The value placed on specialist curriculum strengths has resulted in the appointment of teachers with expertise in technology and science, which has added a rich dimension to school programmes.

Jann's second strategy was to require that staff regularly move around within the school. Initially this proved unpopular, as staff were reluctant to share ideas and resources and many had become professionally comfortable in a familiar niche. Jann challenged this by using her authority to move staff to match student needs and to utilise staff members' skills, expertise and resources. Staff were supported in this transition with side-by-side staff exchanges once a week, with a focus on creating a genuinely collaborative whole-school identity and culture. Requiring all staff to work across the school in response to students' needs has resulted in significant professional development and school-wide consistency in the delivery of quality practice.

A third strategy was to ensure school-wide consistency, and to follow this through in planning and delivery. This was achieved by having a curriculum supervisor oversee all teaching plans, conduct regular visits to the base and satellite classrooms, and give feedback and quality assurance on planning delivery. This is viewed positively by staff, because it links directly to whole-staff brainstorming planning sessions, and to the management of rosters for extensive teacher-aide support and safety through carefully monitored risk management systems.

Another deliberate strategy was to take full control of the budget. Initially, distribution of funds among satellite units tended to be inequitable with regard to discretionary budget and resourcing. Strict protocols have since been developed for spending. Staff can request any resources they require, accompanied by a rationale for purchase. Jann has authority from the board of trustees to spend within a generous budget, and a resource manager ensures that purchases are made quickly.

Jann strongly believes that funding should benefit the children for whom it is intended, and this is reflected in a rapid growth in resources since her arrival. All resources are now centralised, and careful school-wide planning is conducted on an ongoing basis to determine how they are used and to ensure equitable allocation. Recent examples of resource development include a specialist classroom for autistic spectrum disorder students, the expansion of the Bridge Pa site to include a dedicated enviro-classroom, and the building of a therapeutic spa for students with severe physical disability. Wherever possible, students are involved in property or resource decisions, such as in the case of the Bridge Pa ramp. Having identified access as a barrier to their learning, the students discussed ways to fix the problem and then constructed models according to structural and aesthetic considerations. The students presented these to Jann and, at her suggestion, sought quotes for building the ramp, moving fences and the driveway, and for resurfacing the limestone driveway.

A further leadership decision has been to ensure student autonomy. Recently, an able student with Asperger's syndrome, who had been stood down from a local school for his extreme violence towards other students, wanted to attend Fairhaven School. However, as an able student he was not entitled to additional support or funding. In this situation a service agreement is typically reached between the Ministry of Education and both schools to ensure the well-being and continued education of the student. In this case it was decided that the student would be interviewed by his potential classmates in the secondary satellite classroom and that their views would be taken seriously. It was felt that their input should be sought, because the students and staff would be directly affected by his joining the class. The students had a kindly disposition, had developed a protective and safe culture within their group and were enjoying academic success, so it was imperative to involve them in making a decision that could have an impact upon them.

In another successful leadership initiative, Jann implemented quality learning circles to further enhance collaboration, and professional discussion and learning among staff. The focus of each circle is first identified by the group, then readings are shared and discussed at weekly meetings, and strategies are developed to implement new teaching and learning ideas. One recent focus has been the development of staff and student e-portfolios, and the promotion of electronic communication among students and the parent community. It is clear that each of Jann's leadership strategies has been underpinned by an ethos of empowering both staff and students.

The constant learning, refining, regrouping and moving forward is a process that takes energy and personal strength

Key challenges

Making a quantum leap from managing to leading has been a significant challenge for Jann. It is, of course, a journey that has a destination but for which there is no arrival point. The constant learning, refining, regrouping and moving forward is a process that takes energy and personal strength.

Challenges from outside the school add to the complexity of the leadership task of a principal of a specialist school. A review of the sector means yet again having to wait in limbo for crucial Ministry of Education decisions that may directly affect all of those associated with Fairhaven School. The regular uncertainty in relation to political stances on special education can exasperate and demoralise those committed to working with students with disabilities.

The most significant challenges coming from inside the school relate to the management of staff and to the education and well-being of students. Owing to the nature of special education the death of a student is not an infrequent event, but it is one that affects staff and students deeply. The intense level of student care over time means that Fairhaven staff come to know students and their families well. This was evident with the death of a very popular student, whose mischievous personality had delighted staff and classmates alike. Another student was struck by a car while running along the local expressway out of school hours. At the time Jann explained to a curious media that the student's severe autism made it very difficult to keep him safe. Her observation that he "loved to feel the wind in his hair—he would have been enjoying himself" gave comfort to his family and to the many others who were grieving for him. Working in this environment takes a special resilience and dedication.

Sustainable leadership

Having a sense of humour and not taking herself too seriously are fundamental to Jann's resilience. She is adamant that the school comes first. Knowing that she is doing her best and that she is fair, honest and, above all, true to herself adds to this resilience. Jann says that because of her 1940s upbringing, where "rules were rules", honesty with herself and with others is paramount. At Fairhaven Jann feels part of a whole, and ensuring that the whole (the school) will continue strongly without her fulfils her and feeds that resilience.

Jann's support comes from many sources—from her family and her staff in particular. Recently an educational facilitator commented to Jann that, having worked with the Fairhaven staff, she realised that "teachers in special education must be smarter than most." This pleased Jann, because she and the board have worked hard to attract strong, well-qualified staff who are given every opportunity to grow professionally. In turn, staff respect Jann and appreciate the quality of their professional development.

Jann has a network of principal colleagues, including many in the special education environment, who provide invaluable support. Because of the vagaries of the special education sector, and the need for collective strength in advocating for their students, a strong professional network has developed among these principals. The support of the chair of the board of trustees is also critical for Jann, as the current chair brings an objective balance that allows her to make fair and sound leadership decisions.

Personal and professional satisfactions

Success is celebrated daily at Fairhaven, and rather than there being a particular key accomplishment of which she is most proud, Jann feels that the triumphs are ongoing. Seeing the growth of the flourishing learning community at Fairhaven and the students' increasing personal and physical resilience is a very satisfying experience for Jann. The Fun Friday held twice a term, where the whole school, including the satellite classes, meet together with the families, is another ongoing highlight.

Conclusion

Although her base school is the hub, Jann sees the satellite classrooms as offering the best of both worlds, because they provide an opportunity for students with special needs to socialise with their peers and to receive appropriate specialised support. Fairhaven has a welcoming ethos, presents itself as a "normal", attractive school and is clearly an inviting place to be. Nonetheless, some parents still perceive a stigma associated with having their child attend a special school. Jann's unequivocal vision for the future is that special schools be seen by all—parents, staff, students, Ministry of Education and the general public—as a legitimate part of the school system, fully recognised for the valuable contribution they make to New Zealand society.

Reflections for readers

Jann's story documents key influences that have resulted in the collaborative leadership style evident in her current practice. You might like to consider the following reflective questions in consideration of your own practice:

- What themes have there been in your own journey that have been key building blocks in your current leadership model/style. What and who have influenced you in *your* journey?
- Making deep changes within an educational institution affects all the people associated with it. Teaching staff may be particularly challenged by change. Consider the significant changes that have been implemented within your school or centre. Reflect on their impact and degree of success. What have you learned in the change management process?

- In this chapter Jann's leadership strategies have been articulated and are underpinned by an ethos of empowering staff and students. Try listing your own leadership strategies, and consider the principles that underpin what you do and how you do it.
- Challenges can come from both within and outside the school or centre. Examine the internal and external challenges you face and identify the key personal and professional networks that support and sustain you.
- Jann has a vision of sustainability for her own school and a vision of achieving a position of legitimacy for special schools within the New Zealand education sector. Consider your personal vision for your own school or centre, and its future directions.

Suggested further reading

Belasco, J. (1990). *Teaching the elephant to dance: The manager's guide to empowering change.* New York, NY: Crown Publications.

Boyce, M. E. (1996). Organisational story and story telling: A critical review. *Journal of Organisational Change Management, 9*(5), 5–6.

Clandinin, J. D., & Connelly F. M. (1998). Stories to live by: Narrative understandings of school reform. *Curriculum Inquiry, 28*(2), 149–164.

Fullan, M., & Stiegelbauer, S. M. (1991). *The new meaning of educational change* (2nd ed.). New York, NY: Ontario Institute for Studies in Education, Teachers College Press, Teachers College Columbia University.

Harris, A. (2008). *Distributed school leadership.* London, UK: Routledge.

Jenlink, P. M., Reigeluth, C. M., Carr, A. A., & Nelson, L. M. (1998). Guidelines for facilitating systemic change in school districts. *Systems Research and Behavioral Science, 15*, 217–233.

Leithwood, K., Mascall, B., & Strauss, T. (Eds.). (2009). *Distributed leadership according to the evidence.* New York, NY: Routledge.

Lovett, S., & Verstappen, P. (2004). Improving teachers' professional learning: The quality learning circle approach. *New Zealand Journal of Educational Leadership, 19*(2), 31–43.

Phillips, G. (1993). *The school-classroom culture assessment.* Vancouver, British Columbia: Eduserv, British Columbia School Trustees Publishing.

Senge, P. M. (1990). *The fifth discipline: The art and practice of the learning organization.* New York, NY: Currency Doubleday.

Sharken, S. J., with Donovan, J. T. (2001). *5 life stages of non-profit organizations.* St Paul, MN: Wilder Foundation.

Spedding, S. (1996). Teachers as change agents. In P. Foreman (Ed.), *Integration and inclusion in action* (pp. 341–372). Sydney, NSW: Harcourt Brace.

Wagner, C. (2000, October). *School culture analysis.* Paper presented at the Annual Meeting of the Manitoba Association of Resource Teacher (MART), Winnipeg, Manitoba, Canada.

CHAPTER 8

A Holistic Approach to Leading a School

Annie Henry

Larry Ching
Principal, Awatapu College (1996–2002)
Principal, Waimea College (2002–present)

Introduction

What motivates principals to be successful leaders? Why do they sometimes move into roles that are untenable? What do *they* consider to be their key accomplishments as well as their main challenges? Do they separate their personal and professional senses of satisfaction? To what extent does reflection influence their success? More importantly, how do they sustain that success? In this chapter these questions were asked of a secondary principal to gain insight into what it means to become and remain a successful leader within a holistic approach to leading a school.

What motivates a principal?

Larry Ching has served as the principal of Waimea College in Richmond, Nelson for 9 years. When he first arrived at the school a divided staff, declining enrolment and lacklustre support from the community were some of the major challenges Larry faced as the new principal. Within the first 3 to 5 years at Waimea College he had reversed the direction the school was headed. Currently it has more than 1,400 students, 300 more than when Larry arrived, and enrolment is still growing. The challenges have also shifted from changing a culture of what Larry described as "just enough is good enough", improving teaching practices, and building unity and community, to increasing opportunities for more student leadership and expanding the campus.

Every school has its own culture, which is reflected in the values and beliefs that underpin its daily operations (Milstein & Henry, 2008). The culture that exists now at Waimea College is embodied in this section of the school's mission statement:

> We foster a positive environment and encourage leadership, responsibility, self-discipline, positive interaction and healthy competition. Our aim is to help students develop into genuinely friendly and helpful people. Courtesy and honesty are qualities we come to expect from all our students. (Waimea College website, 28 October 2010)

When Larry first spoke with the staff nearly 9 years ago about expecting more from the students, they thought he was criticising their teaching practices. However, by developing a relationship of trust with his staff he was able to communicate the real message behind what he was saying, which was "I wonder if our expectations could be higher?" It was this question that evolved into actions that changed the culture of the school to one of striving to achieve excellence. Other critical building blocks in this transformation included creating leadership opportunities for students, such as selecting academic captains, establishing a high-quality gifted programme, creating an enterprise programme, and growing the arts, music and athletic programmes.

I wonder if our expectations could be higher?

The leadership that Larry and his leadership team provide supports the current school culture. For example, the Year 13 academic captains decide how they will lead. At first student leaders worked individually. Now they set up leadership teams that work to help other students to become positive leaders within the school. This has been achieved by providing planned training and support for students and the educators who serve as their mentors. As a result, the student leadership scheme has evolved from a handful of students applying for the positions into a highly contested process.

Larry's motivation is to bring about positive change. When he arrived at Waimea College he believed that he wanted "to be in a position where I thought I could influence change more … have more of an influence on learning that takes place within the school." Larry is very clear about what needs to happen with regard to student learning. He acknowledges that you have to be heard to make a difference, and be willing to hear others. Staff, students and parents can influence him—not easily, as he admits, but it can happen. It is important to have a culture where people agree on the direction education is headed and understand their influence and role. Then the learning and culture can be reshaped.

What were the key accomplishments?

Larry takes greatest pride in having changed the culture of the school by improving academic performance, extending the range of co- and extra-curricular opportunities, and increasing the support of the community, particularly through parents coaching or managing sports teams, such as the school's 22 netball teams. As Larry observes, "it's a big commitment, but it makes a huge difference to what your school is like."

Another accomplishment is having a clear vision of the teaching and learning practices that need to be instituted to increase student achievement. Teachers now examine and share their teaching and learning strategies more openly than before. For example, at a daily staff meeting a teacher was observed presenting a PowerPoint presentation of the salient points he had gleaned from a recent seminar. The staff then discussed the relevant points while having a cup of tea during their morning break time.

These changes in teachers' practices have also led to improved student achievement. A major outcome of a focused enquiry into teaching and learning is that the school has moved from being below other decile 8 schools in the area to now consistently performing above those at a national level. The school is the second-highest-performing school in the local area in national qualifications, with the exception of a single-sex girls' school. Waimea College girls are achieving at a level higher than other schools in the area. The boys at Waimea College are achieving results at a higher level than they were 5 years ago, when teachers started monitoring the achievement data.

In terms of co- and extra-curricular activities, the school now offers around 80 different options, with the majority of the students involved. Activities are created in response to student needs. In other words, the decisions about which activities to include are not solely the responsibility of the leadership team. Anyone can add an activity. Larry's philosophy is, "If you want it, we'll try and provide it."

Larry feels it is important to attend as many of the activities as possible and spends approximately 80 hours a week involved in the school (Henry, 2009).

Building positive relationships is the crux of everything that happens at the school

He speaks with passion about attending school functions, which, for him, are exciting and fun. As a result staff, students, parents and community see the genuine care he has for everyone in the school, and their relationships with him are strengthened.

The positive, caring, trusting relationships that have developed among students, staff, parents and the community are an evident accomplishment. Building positive relationships is the crux of everything that happens at the school. The system that works best for Larry is to articulate his ideas clearly so that he can be heard, and to set up opportunities for others to be heard. Effective communication and support continue to be important factors in the school's ongoing improvement.

Is personal satisfaction separate from professional satisfaction?

Professional and personal satisfaction are meshed together for Larry. He finds a great deal of personal satisfaction from his professional accomplishments. He is very proud of the students' achievements, how the staff work together to challenge the students to do their best, and the willingness of the community to support the school.

Professional and personal satisfaction are meshed together for Larry

Larry divides his accomplishments into two categories: individual projects and school highlights. One individual project that he worked on for 7 years was the building of a new gymnasium, which was completed in November 2010. This was a lengthy process of securing resources from a range of different places and maintaining support for the project throughout. Now complete, the gymnasium can accommodate a whole host of activities that were not possible before.

Another area where Larry garners satisfaction is the school enrolment, which has increased every year since he arrived. The fact that enrolment has increased by more than 300 students in the past 8 years has also meant the school's staffing and facilities requirements have increased. Gaining approval for facility changes has been relatively easy, but with the current enrolment projection of 1,500, additional facilities will be needed. The question now is, how large should the school be?

Another school highlight has been improved teaching and learning strategies. For example, Waimea College is currently seen as the regional leader of the Education for Enterprise programme. As Larry remarks, "Students built a website with a commercial client and built it around gaining their qualifications as well … It is making education real for them." Larry expands on this in discussing teaching and learning:

> One of the things that has always been a kind of irritation for me is we teach stuff without kids often understanding why. If you can make it meaningful for them, it makes such a difference. The simple formula I use is attendance + engagement = achievement. If you get kids here in the first place, you get them engaged in what they're going to be doing and their level of achievement will take care of itself. But if you don't have

those three things in the mix, if you've got problems with kids with truancy, then how can you get them engaged?

The impact of the Education for Enterprise programme extends beyond teaching and learning strategies. Approximately 75 percent of the students and staff are involved in the programme "because they want to be." This is a huge leap from the small number of students that started working with the programme when it began a few years ago.

Larry gets personal satisfaction from the students' achievements and their amazing accomplishments. He says that:

> I've never woken up in the morning and thought I don't want to go to work. And yet I've had some really busy days ahead of me. But I just like teenagers and I like the kids at this school in particular. We have a nice blend of rural and urban kids.

He then mentions his pleasure in receiving an email from a parent about the school's quiz night and how the students were great ambassadors for the school. This was "a real buzz because it gives you that resilience for when you get the phone call from a parent who's got everything wrong in life and wants to blame you and everyone on your staff for it."

What does it mean to be a school principal?

Larry's response to this question was eloquently stated:

> It's an opportunity to set a kind of dream in place ... if you like. The flash word is a vision, but you know, looking from the outside and thinking what is it that I would like to see available for young people that could improve their lot, either in terms of qualification or becoming active participants in their community. So for me, being a principal means having an opportunity to be a big player in what you can provide for young people.

What are the challenges for a principal?

Larry identifies seven challenges he is currently addressing. The one that causes him the most frustration is the growth of the school and the facilities planning that is needed to meet the projected enrolment of 1,500 in 2011. The frustration comes from having to devote more time to facilities planning than to being an instructional leader, a role he much prefers.

The next major challenge is accommodating staff and student needs, and maintaining the caring community that Larry believes is an essential part of the fabric of the school:

The challenges that go with that are still having that caring community and not allowing it to get too distant—staff and students to get too distant from each other. So that the kid that's out there and is having problems knows where to go easily to get some assistance whether it's academic problems or more emotional types of problems.

The third challenge is meeting subject demands and finding quality staff to teach those subjects. The main problem is to avoid having an oversupply of staff in one area and an undersupply in another, and non-transferable skills for others. For example, more English teachers will be needed next year, but business studies will see a drop in student enrolments. These teachers may need to retrain before they can obtain another position because of supply and demand. To ensure he has quality of instruction, Larry tries to secure needed teachers early, instead of waiting until later in the year.

A fourth challenge relates to a recent event. For the first time since he arrived 9 years ago there was a teacher strike. Larry supports the teachers wanting to have their employment contracts settled, but he feels the timing is not the best because end-of-year exams take place during the stoppage. He also feels that if the Ministry of Education had settled the issue the strike may have been unnecessary:

> I find that quite difficult in my own head when I'm the person that has to keep the school open and keeps it running. And if you've got a limited number of non-union members, then that can create quite a pressure.

A fifth challenge is staying healthy. There have been three student deaths during his years at the school. One was a suicide, another dropped dead on the basketball court and another died as a result of an accident. Some staff members have lost partners or have had major illnesses such as a stroke. There has been a great deal of emotion surrounding each of these tragic events. For Larry, "You kind of just cope with it as you go along. But when you look back, you realise how draining it's been at the time, not just for me but for a whole lot of other people as well, wrapping support round that."

The turnover of board of trustees' members is a sixth challenge. With five of the six members newly elected the previous year, it has been difficult building leadership capacity among the board and providing the training they require for their roles, such as participating in suspension hearings. Fortunately the chairperson has stayed on, so the leadership, experience and institutional knowledge she brings to the board have been retained.

To put everything in perspective, Larry utilises the support of his family—mainly his wife—as well as the school leadership team. He describes his wife as having an uncanny sense for knowing when something is troubling him and then helps him either resolve the issue or put it in the proper context. Because of this support, he is able to deal with the complexity of the issues he faces. He further describes his job as "a lifestyle and they're [his family] very accepting of that."

Larry understands the importance of support—who gives it and how it helps him. He also values reflective practice. He saves a block of time, usually an hour each day, to reflect on his work or to visit classrooms. He refers to this in his diary as "Larry time." His reflective practice takes less time than it did in the past due to being more knowledgeable about his job, having more patience, and engaging in professional development, where he opens himself to new ideas.

> *Larry understands the importance of support—who gives it and how it helps him*

How does a principal sustain success?

Larry focuses on building and keeping positive relationships with his family, students, staff and community. He does this by letting himself "hang out warts and all sometimes." His door is always open. However, when there is a need to close the door, his visitors know that they will receive quality time without interruption.

Larry believes in keeping healthy and fit. He has interests outside the school, such as fishing, woodworking, gardening and drinking quality wine. These are outlets that he sees as stimulating his creative side and "balancing how you see things." Being connected with his family also keeps him healthy. He describes his grandchildren as being a great leveller in his life: "The young ones tell you when they are bored with something and you have to be creative to continue having fun." He also describes his mother as an influence in his well-being and resilience: "There's some role modelling that's been in my background for a long time that helps with that resilience."

Although the relationship with the community is not something Larry talks a great deal about, he recognises that it is vital to the health and well-being of the school. He sees the community as part of the school, and vice versa. It is not just about the school asking the community for support; it is also what the school can give to the community. Personally, he does most of his shopping locally to support the local businesses. They give to the school and he supports them.

Another way Larry builds and strengthens relationships with parents and the community is to return telephone calls as soon as possible, preferably within a day, even if it is only to set up a time to talk. Larry finds that writing letters of thanks, making telephone calls, waving to people as he drives or walks by, and taking the time to listen are how he makes those connections. He has seen a $20,000 donation to a school project as a result of strengthening the school's connections with the community. It is not something he planned, and the donation was not expected. It was an outcome of his genuine care.

Larry charts his own growth by reflecting on his principalship at Waimea College. Maintaining balance has been more difficult, and he is considering having a supervisor or mentor to examine this issue with him. He is constantly finding situations where he can grow, such as the year's theme for the school, "Open to opportunity." He feels he needs to be open. It also means that he is attuned to his own needs. For this reason he feels the leadership structure at the school requires further adaptation:

> If I wish to maintain good contact with staff and students, then I'll have to restructure the way the management team operates here. And obviously I've given it quite a bit of thought and discussed it with the group over the last 12 months in particular. So that will definitely change. And that may be an opportunity, of course, to revert back to some of that more instructional leadership stuff.

Increased enrolment can shift the balance of power within a school. New teachers share their new ideas and excitement and pass on teaching practices to the established staff, which, in turn, improves their work. However, if the new staff are not grounded in the school, their ideas and excitement may not be accepted as readily. New staff members are grounded through the induction process Larry established, and through the leadership team working with the new staff to induct them into the school culture. Similar to leadership or programme development, Larry finds that ensuring people have the necessary background and skills continues to be a major factor in improving academic performance.

What has he learned from the principalship?

Larry reiterates that people know what he stands for, his values and his beliefs. He pursues different avenues to ensure this message is heard. Modelling what you believe sends a clear message: "You shouldn't expect someone to do something that you're not willing to do yourself." Likewise, "you need to know what you're asking and expecting of someone else." Change does not happen overnight. Larry understands that during change there will be periods of little movement, where you have to hold strong to your belief that this is the best thing to do for the school. When the shift begins, it makes the waiting worthwhile.

It is easy to be office bound, which is something Larry acknowledges. He uses his time in the office wisely so that he can be in the classroom or working with people. He has set up systems that help to keep him moving forward. One is not handling paper. For instance, if he meets with someone who has brought along different agenda items, each item is discussed, decisions are made about the appropriate action that needs to be taken, and then the person either takes care of it or gives it to the appropriate person. Notes are taken when days are too full to remember the items that need following up.

Larry has learnt to know his boundaries and he articulates them clearly. As an example, he describes a parent stopping him while he was at the market to question him about school. He asked the parent to ring him on Monday to set up an appointment, when they would have the time to talk. He feels school issues should be discussed at school. When he has stepped over those boundaries by trying to attend all school activities, his leadership team and/or family quickly let him know:

> I get horrendously busy and I feel like I need to be at a whole load of things. But again, I've found along the way that my management team, for example, says, 'For goodness sake, you're not going out to that thing tomorrow night are you? Give it a break.' And I'll stop and think to myself, hmmm. Or they'll say, 'You've been to the last three, why don't I do this one,' or something like that. And my wife's quite good at saying to me, 'Are you sure? Do you really need to be there?'

Larry knows that he has good, capable people around him. He sees that his role has moved from handling day-to-day business to being more of a mentor:

> I spend less time with nuts and bolts stuff and more time with that visionary leadership ... that will necessitate a change in the role ... My role will become an important mentoring and coaching role, helping them to do those changes.

Conclusion

All secondary schools have the potential to be places where innovation and a holistic approach to education can be combined to create learning communities that support everyone involved. This is how Waimea College is seen through the eyes of its principal, leadership team, staff, students, parents and community. However, this was not how the school functioned when Larry Ching took over as principal 9 years ago. Over these years he has created a common goal of promoting and sustaining a school in which everyone is motivated to do their best and sustain a high level of achievement.

Reflections for readers

Holistic leadership is based on the premise that leaders are able to see the larger picture while attending to the details. This split view enables them to adjust to different circumstances while taking in all facets of the organisation's culture. As

Taggart (2011) argues, "Of particular significance is to understand the importance of the whole and the inter-relationships among the components and their elements" (p. 1). It is not merely managing a school: it is building relationships and focusing on what the community can do to support the growth and development of its young people.

In order for leadership to be effective and sustainable, school principals must be resilient and build resiliency in others. Based on Milstein and Henry's (2008) resiliency model, which encompasses the six elements of "positive connections; clear, consistent, and appropriate boundaries; life guiding skills; nurture and support; purposes and expectations; and meaningful participation" (pp. 11–12), Waimea College shows clear evidence of being resilient. Larry Ching has developed *positive connections* within the school, and between the school and the larger community. He recognises his personal *boundaries*, which is a strong model for the leadership team, staff, students and parents. Through the extra-curricular and co-curricular activities, students are learning important *life-guiding skills* of communication, collaboration, mediation and leadership.

With regard to *nurture and support*, Larry is people-centred. Care and support of others is the essence of the school. This was seen through the positive, caring and trusting relationships he has built within the school and its community. A caring environment exists at Waimea College and is essential to Larry. When people have a common purpose, it is much easier for them to work towards the same goals. Having clear *purposes and expectations* is seen in the questions Larry asks of his staff and the direction he leads the school.

The last element is *meaningful participation*. Students, staff, parents and to a lesser degree the community are all engaged with learning. Larry's belief is that "attendance plus engagement equals achievement." Engagement is academic, and also social and emotional. Academic engagement is seen through the accomplishments of the students and staff and a high academic ranking for the school. There are clear indicators that student achievement is on an upwards spiral. The converse is that if someone at Waimea College is hurting in some way, others feel it and respond with care and support. Opportunities for meaningful participation are created.

Durlak, Weissberg, Dymnicki, Taylor and Schellinger (2011) recently conducted a study comparing the results of academically focused schools with schools that have a focus on positive social and emotional support and well-being. They found the schools that focused on positive social and emotional support and well-being performed as well as those schools with only a focus on academic work. One of the clear messages that comes from the Waimea College principal study is one of care, and that "enough isn't good enough." Larry Ching models and lives his beliefs that care and support are vital to the growth and well-being of students and staff. He also attends to his own well-being so that he can be resilient for those connected with the school. Successful leaders are resilient.

Questions for reflection following this case study:

- To what extent do you think Larry's leadership approach matches your own? Are there important differences?
- Do you see yourself as a change agent? If so, what are some of the important changes you have made in schools during your career?
- What strengths do you see in Larry's leadership? Would these be strengths that all successful educational leaders should have?
- Daily reflection on leadership practice is part of one's skill development. How often do you reflect on your leadership role and in what ways has it made a difference?

Suggested further reading

Jaworski, J., & Senge, P. M. (2011). *Synchronicity: The inner path of leadership.* San Francisco, CA: Berrett-Koehler Publishers.

Kouzes, J. M., & Posner, B. Z. (1995). *The leadership challenge: How to keep getting extraordinary things done in organizations.* San Francisco, CA: Jossey-Bass Publishers.

Milstein, M., & Henry, D. A. (2008). *Leadership for resilient schools and communities.* Thousand Oaks, CA: Corwin Press.

Senge, P. M., Cambron-McCabe, N. H., Lucas, T., & Kleiner, A. (2000). *Schools that learn: A fifth discipline fieldbook for educators, parents, and everyone who cares about education.* Auckland: Doubleday.

Senge, P., Kleiner, A., Roberts, C., Ross, R. B., & Smith, B. J. (1994). *The fifth discipline fieldbook: Strategies and tools for building a learning organization.* Auckland: Doubleday.

Ylimaki, R. M., & Jacobson, S. L. (Eds.). (2011*). US and cross-national policies, practices, and preparation: Implications for successful instructional leadership, organizational learning and culturally responsive practices.* Dordrecht, The Netherlands: Springer Press.

References

Durlak, J. A., Weissberg, R. P., Dymnicki, A. B., Taylor, R. D., & Schellinger, K. B. (2011). The impact of enhancing students' social and emotional learning: A meta-analysis of school-based universal interventions. *Child Development, 82*(1), 405–432.

Henry, D. A. (2009). Moving a school from division to unity. *Journal of Educational Leadership, Policy, and Practice, 24*(1), 16–20.

Milstein, M. M., & Henry, D.A. (2008). *Leadership for resilient schools and communities.* Thousand Oaks, CA: Corwin Press.

Taggart, J. (2011). *Holistic leadership.* Retrieved 28 March 2011, from http://EzineArticles.com/ 2490145.

CHAPTER 9

Whānau Leadership in Early Childhood

Kate Thornton

Hinerangi Korewha
Kaitiaki, Te Kōpae Piripono
(1994–present)

Aroaro Tamati
Kaitiaki, Te Kōpae
Piripono (1994–present)

Introduction

This leadership story explores the collective and collaborative leadership practised at Te Kōpae Piripono, a Māori immersion early childhood education centre situated in New Plymouth. The chapter focuses on the Māori concept of whānau (family) and on the role of the kaitiaki (teacher) in fostering a learning community where everyone is a leader and everyone's contribution matters. This form of leadership can be termed whānau leadership, because all whānau members are encouraged to contribute to and be involved in leadership within the Kōpae. The chapter begins with a brief description of the history of Te Kōpae Piripono and the service it provides. This is followed by an account of the model of leadership developed at Te Kōpae Piripono and a discussion of the role of the kaitiaki in fostering this collective and collaborative whānau leadership practice.

Background

Te Kōpae Piripono was established in 1994 as part of a move to support the reclamation of Māori language and identity in the Taranaki region. The centre provides a Māori immersion early childhood education programme for approximately 25–30 children. According to a research report published as part of the centre's participation in the Ministry of Education-funded Centres of Innovation programme, Te Kōpae Piripono was

> born out of a shared desire to rear our children on kaupapa Māori, that is within a Māori paradigm, speaking the language of their forebears, and at home with indigenous concepts and practices. (Tamati, Hond-Flavell, Korewha, and Whānau of Te Kōpae Piripono, 2008, p. 2)

Leadership practice

The two kaitiaki interviewed for this chapter are Aroaro Tamati and Hinerangi Korewha, both of whom are registered early childhood teachers, founding whānau members and the current directors (tumu) of Te Kōpae Piripono. Leadership at Te Kōpae Piripono is not, however, restricted to those in formal positions. The model of whānau leadership means there is an expectation that everyone at the centre, including whānau and children, is involved in leadership. Aroaro emphasises the need to be continually conscious of how leadership is enacted and to continually look for opportunities to acknowledge leadership in others. She believes that this heightened consciousness plays an essential role in fostering leadership among all those who are part of the centre, "because when we start acknowledging the leadership in the children who come here and that of their extended families, it's then that we ourselves can truly learn and grow as leaders."

Aroaro emphasises the need to be continually conscious of how leadership is enacted and to continually look for opportunities to acknowledge leadership in others

In 2005 Te Kōpae Piripono began participating in a 3-year Centre of Innovation research project funded by the Ministry of Education. Focusing on leadership practice and whānau development, the study explored the following research question: "How does whānau development at Te Kōpae Piripono foster leadership, across all levels, to enhance children's learning and development?"

Here, whānau is an inclusive concept that does not distinguish between parents, children, teachers and management. According to the research report, "whānau development involves the learning and development of every member of our community of learners" (Tamati et al., 2008, p. 8). Participation in the project has enabled Te Kōpae Piripono to develop a clear sense of their leadership practice, which they express through a framework, Ngā Takohanga e Whā, based on the precious to them. This is the first point of trust. So it needs to be reciprocated with some type of warm acknowledgement and action— basically saying you are welcome, this is a place for you to belong.

Making whānau feel comfortable and, eventually, confident in participating as leaders at Te Kōpae Piripono takes time and is seen as the responsibility of the kaitiaki. Aroaro describes this process as follows:

> These are the things we do, we greet each other warmly, they are basic things, and we make sure that no one is left out and anything to do with speaking harshly to each other is left to the side. All these sorts of things, these conventions, or ways of doing and being, are things that we have to constantly work at. Not only do many parents coming in have this negative experience and therefore a negative view of education, they also have a sense of powerlessness that they don't actually have a say or any power to advocate for themselves and their children. When you work with that you are dealing with huge amounts of fear and anxiety. So who is going to fill the breach? Who is going to be the bridge to help them through that initial fear, that stumbling point? It's not insurmountable but it feels like it. So who does that? Is the onus on the families to do that? No way! These families are new to the Kōpae. That's totally unrealistic.

Actively and genuinely engaging with whānau involves interacting and connecting with them on a daily basis. The Centre of Innovation study found that the involvement of whānau at Te Kōpae Piripono was directly related to the level of engagement of kaitiaki. The growing confidence of whānau, such as Sheldon, whose story was referred to earlier, is dependent on the persistence of kaitiaki, "especially with those who are visibly most uncomfortable." It also involves "shifting people's thinking to be comfortable and open to the idea of acknowledging their self-worth and that they have much to offer and contribute" (Tamati et al., 2008, p. 112).

Another important element in engaging with whānau is being clear about expectations and involvement. The expectations of whānau involvement are explained to families during the induction process at Te Kōpae Piripono, and new enrolments are limited to families who are willing to support the aims and objectives of the centre. Everyone's contribution to Te Kōpae Piripono is valued and the wider involvement of the community helps build trust and a sense of belonging. One way of involving whānau is to say, "This is the job—who has the skills?" It is accepted that people's involvement will vary in degree and will develop at different rates. Accordingly, Te Kōpae Piripono "recognises that people are at different stages of development. This allows all involved to participate in a way that is most appropriate for them, according to skill, ability and background" (Tamati et al., 2008, p. 4).

While the actual leadership at Te Kōpae Piripono is clearly "distributed", those at the centre prefer to see their leadership structure as whānau-based; they argue that distributed leadership assumes there is someone else who does the distribution. In this regard, the whānau leadership practised at Te Kōpae Piripono is very different from what most people have previously experienced. According to Aroaro, whānau leadership is premised on the idea of takoha, or contribution. People's self-initiated and heart-felt contributions appear to happen naturally within this whānau context. These contributions, Hinerangi adds, are then recognised, acknowledged and woven into the "warp and the weft" of Te Kōpae Piripono.

Aroaro describes how conversations are used to promote this concept of leadership:

> Because the hierarchical leadership norm is an unspoken one where people assume this is how it is, they naturally fall into place in line with that thought, so no one actually says you don't matter or what I say goes; it's all unspoken. What we are trying to do is bring the unspoken to the fore. We actually talk about it, bring it to the table and have the conversation. Because by doing that nothing is off limits. The way is open for people to talk about their hopes, their joys, their dreams and their fears.

These conversations lead to stronger relationships and to greater whānau empowerment. As Aroaro explains, "when people realise they're actually important enough to us to have that conversation, it changes the whole nature of the relationship."

Another key approach to fostering trusting relationships is open and honest communication. The ability to have rigorous and courageous conversations depends on a high level of trust. Therefore, the centre has established a number of agreed processes for open communication, and these are shared with whānau. Examples of these processes include genuinely listening to other people's perspectives, clarifying understanding and intentions, and providing the time and space for others to make their own decisions. In some cases, developing positive and reciprocal relationships involves persistence and can be a long and challenging process. As Aroaro explains:

> To be the glue you sometimes have to have tough conversations. It's actually not all rosy and, to be honest with you, the stronger forged relationships are those where the tough questions have been asked. That takes a considerable amount of courage and leadership.

These robust conversations also happen during the weekly kaitiaki hui (staff meetings). Aroaro describes these discussions as "really deep and meaningful, they are passionate and they're direct. There's no mucking around and talking frivolously, things are too important to be frivolous."

Hinerangi and Aroaro were both asked how they have managed to maintain their motivation and passion for working at Te Kōpae Piripono after so many years.

Hinerangi says that one driving force is knowing they are making a difference in the lives of the whānau, not only in terms of the education of their children, but also in more personal and long-lasting ways:

> It is about the brighter future for tamariki, whānau, hapū and te iwi Māori. You know that you are contributing to restoring balance in people's lives—a sense of peace. When people start experiencing the positiveness within the all-embracing, warm, nurturing environment of the Kōpae, then they have the space and time to gain insight into themselves and the wealth of knowledge and ability they actually have. It is then they start to realise the leadership within them.

Aroaro describes the satisfaction in feeling that you have made a difference in the lives of children and their whānau:

> For me although it's been hard, at times, over the years, the energy that derives from working together and having success—success on a comprehensive scale—and you know the small successes are actually big successes—making that connection with whānau. So it's not a job for me. When you get to working on the same page with whānau, the energy that comes from that is all-embracing. The power within it is so moving, it has a life of its own. How do you tap into that anywhere else?

You know the small successes are actually big successes

Aspirations for the future

Te Kōpae Piripono's strategic plan articulates the future directions agreed on by whānau. These aspirations relate not only to the immediate educational environment but also to the original purpose of Te Kōpae Piripono, which was to reclaim Māori language and identity in the Taranaki region. Aroaro expresses this as follows:

> For us it's all about our culture and our identity as a whānau. Our strategic plan is about strengthening Taranaki reo [the unique Taranaki dialect] and tikanga [customs] of Taranaki so that it can be strengthened throughout the whānau. All of the vision for Kōpae going forward is about our identity as Māori and our connections with whānau, hapū and iwi because, at the end of the day, if we can reach out to make those connections on a wider scale then maybe that will have benefits for a whole lot of other people. That's not being arrogant. It's actually a moemoeā (aspiration).

However, this is not an easy path. It involves a huge commitment on the part of kaitiaki to ongoing whānau development in te reo Māori. Hinerangi notes that sustaining this commitment is a fundamental issue: "If the Kōpae does not find solutions and find critical friends to support this taxing part of our work, then the Kōpae will not be able to sustain itself into the future."

Conclusion

The story of the leadership at Te Kōpae Piripono is inspiring. The concept of whānau leadership has been successfully implemented and supported through a clearly articulated leadership framework. Although this model may not be directly transferable to different educational contexts, others interested in ways of sharing leadership and empowering communities can learn from this collective and collaborative approach. By engaging directly with families, the kaitiaki at Te Kōpae Piripono have managed to encourage whānau to realise their own leadership potential. Ultimately, this has led to the development of a unique educational environment where the children of Te Kōpae Piripono are able to proudly learn and grow as Māori and as fully participating citizens of the world (Tamati et al., 2008).

Reflections for readers

Hinerangi and Aroaro were asked if there were any key aspects of the whānau leadership practised at Te Kōpae Piripono that could be transferred to other settings. Initially they both responded that it was not intended as a template for other settings to copy and that what would work in another setting could look quite different to what works at Te Kōpae Piripono. However, both tumuaki (leaders) then described their approach in ways that leaders in other settings could reflect on. For Hinerangi:

> The easiest term that I think of, about the idea of transferring this to other settings, is 'care for caring's sake', because it's as simple as that. Caring in your establishment will look different to caring in someone else's. But one thing that people can contemplate on is, what are you doing that shows other people you genuinely care about them—which for us is aroha.

For Aroaro:

> It's all about aroha—that is the overarching thing, at the end of the day being a true whānau setting. Te aroha [caring]. Te mahi tahi [working collaboratively]. Aroha is paramount in all of this because through aroha people feel they belong and know that people care about them. People are important.

These comments further support the idea that when hierarchy is taken out of leadership, what remains are people and relationships. At Te Kōpae Piripono it is believed that relationships with others play a central role in what people think and do as leaders. As we reflect on how the notion of whānau leadership could be encouraged in a range of educational settings, we can ask ourselves the questions that Te Kōpae Piripono posed in their research: "What do we need to do to exercise the four responsibilities? And how can we foster a learning community where everyone is a leader and where everyone's contribution matters?" (Te Kōpae Piripono, 2006, p. 8).

Further consideration of the leadership framework referred to earlier in the chapter, and of links to other leadership literature, can also help us to reflect on these questions. Te mouri takohanga (being responsible) relates to an individual's attitude and actions. Being responsible is about being professional, acting ethically and appropriately, being honest, being positive, and being open to others and to different perspectives. This responsibility can be related to the concept of *authentic leadership*. Shamir and Eilam (2005) describe authentic leaders as "leaders whose actions are based on their values and convictions" (p. 397). They also suggest that authentic leaders are characterised by their transparency as "their talk and actions are consistent with their beliefs and values" (pp. 397–398).

Te kawe takohanga (taking responsibility) is about courage, risk-taking, "having a go", taking up the challenge and trying new things. Often people need to be encouraged to take responsibility, and those in formal leadership positions can encourage and support others to have a go through mentoring and coaching, and demonstrating faith in the abilities of others. Te tuku takohanga (sharing responsibility) is about sharing power, roles and positions. It also relates to interacting and engaging with others. This sharing of leadership responsibilities can be related to the three key elements of distributed leadership suggested by Bennett, Wise, Woods and Harvey (2003):

- Leadership is an emergent property of a group of individuals who interact, rather than an individual phenomenon.
- The boundaries of leadership are open and fluid.
- Different types of expertise are distributed across many rather than a few.

The three responsibilities discussed above can also be related to two of the aspects of leadership knowledge, skills and dispositions identified in the *School Leadership and Student Outcomes* best evidence synthesis: building relational trust and engaging in open-to-learning conversations (Robinson, Hohepa, and Lloyd, 2009). The importance of building trust with whānau has been discussed in an earlier section and is a prerequisite for encouraging others to participate in leadership. The determinants of relational trust outlined in the best evidence synthesis include interpersonal respect, personal regard for others, competence in role and personal integrity (Robinson et al., 2009). Engagement in open-to-learning conversations is characterised by "clear and open disclosure of one's point of view, explicit checking and requests for feedback, and detecting and checking assumptions" (p. 200). This can be linked to the rigorous and courageous conversations described in an earlier section of the chapter and is a necessary prerequisite for whānau leadership.

Te whai takohanga (having responsibility) relates to having designated roles and positions of responsibility, and is the responsibility most closely aligned with the traditional notion of leadership. Rather than viewing this as the predominant responsibility, it can be seen as "a natural evolution" of the other three responsibilities (Tamati et al., 2008, p. 28). Finally, the interrelationship between the four responsibilities in terms of whānau leadership is explained as follows:

> It is through *having* responsibility and *sharing* responsibility then being encouraged to and supported to *take* responsibility, that whānau members, individually and collectively come to *be* responsible. (Tamati et al., 2008, p. 27).

The following reflective questions are posed for readers:
- How can a learning community, where everyone is a leader and everyone's contribution matters, be fostered in your organisation?
- In what ways in the leadership of children/students encouraged and celebrated?
- How are positive and reciprocal relationships with parents/whanau built? How are they encouraged to participate in the life of your educational workplace?
- What is the relevance of the four responsibilities framework for your personal leadership practice?

Suggested further reading

Gardner, T., Avolio, B., Luthans, F., May, D., & Walumba, F. (2005). Can you see the real me? A self-based model of authentic leader and follower development. *Leadership Quarterly*, 16(3), 581–613.

Garger, J. (2008). Developing authentic leadership in organizations: Some insights and observations. *Development and Learning in Organizations*, 22(1), 14–16.

Lambert. L. (2002). A framework for shared leadership. *Educational Leadership*, April, 17–19.

Spillane, J., Halverson, R., & Diamond, J. (2004). Towards a theory of leadership practice: A distributed perspective. *Journal of Curriculum Studies*, 36(1), 3–34.

Timperley, H. (2005). Distributed leadership: Developing theory from practice. *Journal of Curriculum Studies*, 37(4), 395–420.

References

Bennett, N., Wise, C., Woods, P., & Harvey, J. (2003). *Distributed leadership*. Nottingham, UK: National College for School Leadership.

Education Review Office. (2009). *Te Kōpae Piripono education review report*. Retrieved from http://www.ero.govt.nz/Early-Childhood-School-Reports/Early-Childhood-Reports/Te-Kōpae-Piripono-21-09-2009.

Harris, A. (2004). Distributed leadership and school improvement. *Educational Management Administration and Leadership, 32*(1), 11–24.

Harris, A. (2008). Distributed leadership: According to the evidence. *Journal of Educational Administration, 46*(2), 172–188.

Robinson, V., Hohepa, M., & Lloyd. (2009). *School leadership and student outcomes: Identifying what works and why: Best evidence synthesis iteration.* Wellington: Ministry of Education.

Shamir, B., & Eilam, G. (2005). What's your story? A life-stories approach to authentic leadership development. *Leadership Quarterly, 16*(3), 395–417.

Tamati, A., Hond-Flavell, E., Korewha, H., & Whānau of Te Kōpae Piripono. (2008). *Centre of Innovation Research report of Te Kōpae Piripono.* Retrieved from http://www.education counts.govt.nz/publications/ece/22551/34825/34830.

Te Kōpae Piripono. (2006). *Ngā takohanga e wha: The four responsibilities.* Retrieved from http://www.lead.ece.govt.nz/CentresOfInnovation/COIDocsAndResources/SrvcSpecificDocs AndResources/NgāTakohangaeWhaTheFourResponsibilities.htm.

following four key responsibilities: te whai takohanga (having responsibility); te mauri takohanga (being responsible); te kawe takohanga (taking responsibility); and tuku takohanga (sharing responsibility) (Te Kōpae Piripono, 2006). These responsibilities and associated leadership actions will be discussed in more depth later in the chapter.

Overall, this leadership framework is based on the idea that if the traditional Western hierarchical structure is taken out of the thinking about leadership, then what is left is people and relationships. Accordingly, Ngā Takohanga e Wha is about relationships—among children, kaitiaki and whānau—and the sharing of responsibility, or leadership, through interacting and engaging with others, listening to others' points of view, acknowledging different perspectives, and asking for and providing assistance.

The research report on Te Kōpae Piripono tells a number of different leadership stories involving children, whānau and kaitiaki. Children's leadership is illustrated in a story describing how a child organised a tangi (funeral) for a pet bird and an account of how a group of children worked together to compose a song. A story relating to whānau is about "the role of fathers, fear and the power of positive action" (Tamati et al., 2008, p. 110). In this case, Sheldon, the father of a child at Te Kōpae Piripono, gained confidence through participating in the activities at the centre and was eventually encouraged to contribute his musical talents. Another story discusses a kaitiaki, Kahumako, who had trained as an early childhood teacher but lacked self-belief and confidence when she first arrived at Te Kōpae Piripono. Kahumako explains how her involvement at the centre enabled her to develop the confidence to express her point of view, because it served as "a safe haven" where she could "practise, try new things, make mistakes and learn from them" (Tamati et al., p. 119). These stories illustrate how the inclusive approach to leadership practised at Te Kōpae Piripono provides a space where all can become leaders, especially those who have struggled with inequitable power relationships with educational institutions and in the wider community.

According to a recent Education Review Office report (Education Review Office, 2009), this model of leadership practice has been very successful:

> Whānau, staff and children are supported to be leaders collectively and individually. These groups all demonstrate leadership in numerous ways. Ngā Takohanga e Wha have been developed as local aspects of leadership. That is, to be a leader, to have leadership, to share leadership, and to take the lead. Children are provided with opportunities to take leadership roles that they do willingly and regularly. Parents and Kaitiaki are also well supported and encouraged to take leadership roles. (p. 16)

Greater involvement of whānau in leadership is an exciting concept, which may be relevant to a range of other educational settings. The kaitiaki play a crucial role in fostering this distributed leadership.

Role of the kaitiaki

At Te Kōpae Piripono, the kaitiaki are seen as the "glue" that cements the relationships among those involved in the centre, and they support leadership through whānau development. In this sense, the kaitiaki fulfil a formal leadership role in tying together the different components of the organisation (Harris, 2004). Aroaro believes that this is the responsibility of the kaitiaki, in that it reflects their "very nature of being the constant element at Te Kōpae Piripono." Harris (2008) describes formal leaders as "the gatekeepers to distributed leadership practice" (p. 175) and suggests that they create the conditions under which distributed leadership can flourish. At Te Kōpae Piripono, the kaitiaki foster the distribution of leadership by actively and genuinely engaging with whānau and encouraging sharing in leadership and decision making. Ongoing daily contact with whānau is also seen as important. As Aroaro explains, "we are the glue to those families. We make the connections; we are the connections, the daily contact."

The beginning of that trust is the acknowledgement that the whānau are bringing their most valuable possession, their children

For many of the families joining Te Kōpae Piripono, their previous experience of education has not always been positive. Aroaro and Hinerangi describe some people's perceptions of their own self-worth as like "a tin of fish." As Hinerangi says:

> That's the harsh reality for educational institutions today, that families come in with that view of themselves and the way that some centres and schools operate really reinforces that view and it just gets worse because it's cyclic. We're actually trying to break the cycle.

At Te Kōpae Piripono the kaitiaki work to break this cycle through building strong and trusting relationships with whānau. The beginning of that trust is the acknowledgement that the whānau are bringing their most valuable possession, their children, to Te Kōpae Piripono to learn in a Māori immersion environment. As Hinerangi explains:

> You've got families starting up and in the worst case scenario they don't have much faith in anything but they're willing to trust in terms of bringing their children, because they can identify that they didn't get to learn their own language, but they want that for their children. So they are entrusting us with their children—that which is most

CHAPTER 10

Cultural Change and Moral Leadership

Paul Potaka

Mark Brown
Principal, Waihao Downs School (1985–1988)
Deputy Principal and Principal, Victory School, Nelson (1988–present)

Introduction

The pressure on principals today is greater than ever before. A principal needs to be sensitive to a growing list of staff, student and community needs, build learning communities, give advice and guidance to boards of trustees, ensure the school meets its legislative and legal responsibilities, carry out board of trustees' policies, and provide the initiative and drive that ensures their school continues to move forward.

While this all sounds like an overwhelming and impossible job for one person, it shows the importance placed on the role of the principal in modern schools. It is clear they have an important role in setting and maintaining the direction of the school and ensuring it is a vibrant place of learning. So much for the expectations for principals; but what do principals actually *do*? How do they exercise leadership and mediate the many and often conflicting expectations held for them?

Although the school at the centre of this case study is similar to other schools, it is also different in many ways. The differences have a lot to do with the leadership style, strategies and choices exercised by the principal, who exemplifies moral leadership in action. We see examples of the softer side of leadership (Notman,

2009), with its concern for the community's goals balanced against the expectations of bureaucracy.

Making a difference in the lives of children, teachers and parents is important to this principal. Through this study we obtain an insight into aspects of moral leadership that have transformed the culture of a school from fragmentation and conflict to unification under one vision. We learn why he became a principal, the challenges and dilemmas he faced, his accomplishments, the strategies used, his reflections, and his hopes for the future. In the process we see moral leadership in action as we learn the difference between an ordinary school and a community school, and witness how this principal has ensured that social justice is maintained in a multi-ethnic, low-decile school.

The principal

Mark Brown was appointed principal of Victory School, Nelson, in 1994 after successful experiences as a new entrant and reading recovery teacher, and rural principal. His pre-teaching work experiences included labouring in shearing gangs, freezing works and scrub cutting, which are many of the jobs the members of his community have had. These—together with other life experiences such as divorce, solo fatherhood and employment uncertainty—have all contributed to his ability to relate to, and empathise with, the members of his community.

Various staff and community members describe Mark as energetic, welcoming, committed and passionate about what he does. The school is a busy place and Mark is an action-oriented principal. This was confirmed in my observations of him at work. Mark's positive attitude pervades the school as he interacts with staff and students. He makes time for people, gets on with everyone and establishes good relationships with community agencies. This included entertaining a visit to his office by children who had made significant achievements in their class work, introducing a visiting Chinese delegation to the school and handling daily notices.

Challenges and dilemmas

Many of Mark's challenges stem from community demographics and the need to integrate refugees and new immigrants into the school. This often involves playing a part in reuniting families who have been split in the process of leaving their country of origin. Mark is also keen to ensure Nelson people know the refugees' stories, and that those who work closest with them understand the differences between the various refugee groups.

Mark has intimate knowledge of the families of the children at Victory School and he deals with them on a day-to-day basis. He quickly becomes aware of any issues and is able to step in to provide agencies with advice and guidance about what the families need. Helping to integrate families into the school and the community has become part of the school's "core business." Mark sees this as a necessary precondition for enabling immigrant children to participate in the curriculum.

> Helping to integrate families into the school and the community has become part of the school's "core business"

The ability or inability of many parents to be effective in the role expected of a good parent is a major challenge for the school. The effects of poverty are also a factor for some families, and for the school. Other challenges identified by Mark are households with large numbers of people where family members have few qualifications and houses with large numbers of district health board clients. According to Mark, people who care are the answer to meeting the needs of children and their families—not necessarily money. He has difficulty finding suitable support staff to assist with school programmes, and employing teachers poses a risk because applicants do not always know or appreciate the community, school and philosophy they are being asked to sign up to. Under these circumstances he finds it more rewarding to grow his own staff. Mark recognises the strengths and weaknesses of support agencies as they work to realise the school's expectations and to integrate families and students into the school and community. He works skilfully, diplomatically and, at times, assertively with them to ensure appropriate actions are taken.

Mark's oversight of key issues in education is shown in his concern for the impact that recent initiatives, such as Te Marautanga and Ngā Whanaketanga,[1] will have on his students. He says, "We don't want to penalise our tamariki",[2] and he has made a commitment to familiarise himself with these initiatives to ensure they are successfully implemented in his school. The community is happy with the school's current situation, but Mark believes there is much more that needs to be done to meet his vision of social justice for all members of his community. Success is currently measured in terms of programmes that meet a mixture of student and family health, social and educational needs.

---

1 Te Marautanga is the New Zealand curriculum for Māori immersion and bilingual schools, and Ngā Whanaketanga are the national standards for these schools.
2 Tamariki is a New Zealand Māori word for child or children.

Accomplishments

Mark's first achievement was to deal successfully with the school's changing cultural profile. At one time the school roll was mostly of lower socio-economic status. Today, non-European students make up 80 percent of the school roll: up to one-third are new immigrants, and the school has a significant Māori population, with six bilingual classes.

With a mandate for change, Mark has worked hard to create an environment in which the school and the community embrace these many ethnicities, and individuals and the community share a positive sense of self-belief. Mark's vision is a school underpinned by social justice, where everyone is valued, health and safety are paramount, and everyone can learn and achieve their potential. These were the precursors to Mark's success in changing the negative public perception held about the school and community.

With a mandate for change, Mark has worked hard to create an environment in which the school and the community embrace these many ethnicities, and individuals and the community share a positive sense of self-belief

Mark's key focus has been to articulate and communicate the vision of the school so that it can be heard, seen, known and felt by everyone in the school and community. He strives to convey the message to students, staff and parents that they matter and that they have a role in his vision for the school. Initially this was not something Mark was comfortable with, but he believes he has become better at it over the last 2 to 3 years. He has now become very successful at articulating his vision, to the point where the phrase "Everyone matters at Victory" has become a mantra for staff and students.

His experience with refugees has redefined for him what it means for a school to be safe. He relates how this has been a huge issue for the school and how it is linked to the concept of trust. Refugees in his community have been the victims of displacement, torture, violence, rape and trauma. They have attempted to avoid shame by keeping these issues within their own communities. These experiences have created a need for them to learn again how to trust—to trust themselves and other people, as well as the authorities and institutions in society, including the school.

Many of the refugees in the school community had learned not to discuss their thoughts and opinions with people in authority, such as principals, because this could result in being displaced, shot or imprisoned. Mark has worked hard to ensure refugees see the school as a trusted place, receptive to their needs. This has not come easily, and it has involved learning about the various refugee cultures, proving to them that they can talk freely without fear of repercussions.

By gaining a deeper understanding of his refugee community Mark has managed to reverse a personal "mental disconnect". This has resulted in the school and community goals becoming more closely aligned and better supported. Examples of this support include the establishment of English-language classes, a play group to take care of pre-school children while their mothers attend classes, and a community centre modelling the school ethos to service the community's health, welfare and social needs in a holistic way. This focus on family and community issues has seen the school become a "one-stop shop", where families can readily access health and social services such as parent education, WINZ, midwives, Zumba classes, badminton, and an economic enterprise scheme.

This focus on the welfare of the family as a whole has meant that parents feel more connected to the school. The school premises are also used for music lessons, meeting rooms, orientation programmes and support services for adults. For example, the school has established after-school care facilities to meet the learning and social needs of immigrant children. A Social Worker in Schools representative liaises with the school and relevant agencies to ensure children's issues are dealt with as quickly as possible. Other forms of institutional support are provided by national and local organisations, including the Ministry of Education, University of Canterbury Plus, the Nelson Multi-ethnic Council and various charitable organisations.

Because of these connections, one of Mark's key roles has been to mediate between families and agencies. He has led the charge to unpack, articulate and implement strategies to meet the needs of low-income families, refugees, new immigrants and the Māori community. He has worked alongside various government and local body agencies to help improve families' well-being, including the Ministries of Health and Social Development, the New Zealand Families Commission, the Nelson Marlborough Area Health Board and the Nelson City Council.

Mark's personal focus is clearly on building leadership capacity within his school. He is proud of the professional development opportunities he has created and the fact that several of his staff have been promoted to principals of other schools. He has expanded his leadership team to nine people and created co-leadership at the deputy principal level, in recognition of the complexity of the leadership within the school. His view is that leadership should be exercised by many people in the school. However, the impact of his own leadership is evident, and the feeling of one parent is that Mark has played a critical role in the success of the school: "I think the school is very much a [principal] show but I don't necessarily think that is a bad thing." Mark's success was recognised when he was awarded a Woolf Fisher Scholarship for 2008. This gave him an opportunity to learn about educational leadership in the United States and United Kingdom.

Successful leadership strategies

Mark understands schools and knows his community intimately. He understands the needs of his school and the community, listens to their aspirations, helps them to achieve their goals, forms relationships with individuals and groups within his school and community, and builds partnerships with various agencies to ensure school goals are achieved. His training and experience have taught him what schools are about. He has gained an intimate knowledge of the ethnic and socio-economic composition of his community by meeting community members on their own terms, through cultural celebrations and sport.

Evidence of Mark's relationship building can be seen in the excellent working relationship he has developed with his board of trustees. It is also evident in the widespread camaraderie and cohesion found among staff, who say they would not wish to teach anywhere else. They enjoy teaching at Victory School, have aspirations for their students and are viewed by students and parents as excellent teachers. Mark has created a platform so that everyone has a voice in the school. Every effort is made to ensure people feel included in the democratic processes of the school. Members of the Māori and refugee communities are represented on the board of trustees, and Mark meets with sub-committees under the aegis of "community liaison." In addition, the board has a new chairperson, who brings an academic focus to the board's deliberations. In Mark's words, "She aligns with the core beliefs of the school yet also challenges our assumptions."

It is also evident in the widespread camaraderie and cohesion found among staff, who say they would not wish to teach anywhere else

Mark has worked successfully with staff and the community to build an ethos and identity that have seen a resurgence of pride in self, school and community among everyone associated with the school. This is reflected in the words of one parent who stated, "Whenever I drive up the street and I see the park I think, 'Oh yea! It's home!' It's part of me." This pride was reflected in Mark's community winning the national award for New Zealand Community of the Year in 2009.

Sustaining success

Mark's success has been built on a number of factors, including the effective use of the relevant educational and social agencies and securing their long-term commitment. Sustaining the processes that ensure community voices are heard will continue to be a challenge in this transient community. An open door policy and listening to people have been important, but Mark believes more needs to be done to ensure the school receives regular, timely and relevant feedback to guide future demands.

The key to sustaining success is the support Mark gets from his staff and his board. Staff act out the philosophy of the school each day, and the board provides support in the form of what they do as well as what they say. Importantly, the board restricts its interest to governing and does not interfere in the principal's managerial responsibilities. Mark also finds support for what he does in his professional reading and takes comfort from the research evidence.

Critical self-reflection

The experience Mark gained as the recipient of a prestigious Woolf Fisher Scholarship has done much to help him achieve an improved life–work balance. It has helped him expand his views on what is desirable and possible in a school.

It has also made him reflect on, and question, many of the beliefs he previously held. For example, the question of what constitutes success has made him think about what success might mean in another school context. The educational experience Mark gained overseas has challenged

The educational experience Mark gained overseas has challenged his assumptions and belief systems, and has encouraged him to re-examine the alignment between what he believes and how he acts

his assumptions and belief systems, and has encouraged him to re-examine the alignment between what he believes and how he acts. It has encouraged him to listen more carefully to groups he might not have listened to before. He has become more aware of the importance of detecting tone, and of taking note of how people interact and the types of language they use.

Recently Mark has noticed that negativity has begun to creep into the school and he has taken steps to reverse the trend. Part of his realignment has involved restructuring the leadership team and having them think about where they would like to be in 3 to 4 years' time. Although the number on the team has increased from five to nine, different areas for leadership have been identified, especially of the bilingual classes and to support refugees. Some roles were perceived as being too busy and unmanageable, so tasks have been split and reallocated to make them achievable. This has also reduced the pressure on school leaders in terms of their classroom roles. Mark has even changed the names used to describe the various leadership functions. The leadership team is now described as a leadership forum, to reflect the idea that "we are not managing things—we are leading."

Part of making a difference has involved Mark exercising a greater critique of the school and the work he does. He constantly asks reflective questions of himself and those around him; for instance, "So what? What now? What is the evidence?" This has led to his being more explicit about what he wants for students and teachers in his school.

It is clear from Mark's day-to-day actions that his work is guided by a moral purpose, grounded in issues related to cultural change, social justice, integrating school and community, and making a difference for students in his care. This connection makes Mark's work bold, powerful, challenging and rewarding. It has involved helping people find and express their voice, listening to people, and changing the way they think about themselves, their community and their school. It has meant helping people believe they have a future.

In recent years Mark has made time to think and reflect on what it means for him to be a leader. He has come to the realisation that he needs to have balance in his life and that he needs to take care of himself to be able to continue to take care of other people. Mark has willingly invested a lot of time and energy into his school and community, but he believes that now might be a good time to take care of some of his own needs. While he thoroughly enjoys his work, he also aspires to travel and engage in more formal study. For one thing, he has a Bachelor of Education degree that he wants to upgrade.

Strategies for making a difference

Mark strives to make a difference in the lives of his students and their families. He says there was "a conscious decision to change [the] culture within the school." When he first arrived at the school he found an underlying dysfunction in the relationships between home and school, and student and teacher. In addition, the school and the community were not supportive of student engagement in learning. Initially Mark needed to act in a fire-fighting mode. This has changed as he has become more proactive in working collaboratively with others who have the relevant knowledge and skills. This, in turn, has sped the improvement process for families and made Mark less central to individual cases.

One initiative that helped turn things around was a programme called Eliminating Violence. This involved collecting data that highlighted behavioural dysfunction within the school. While staff at the time felt this was okay, new staff wanted to improve behaviour in the school. Accordingly, the school embarked on a new way forward, based on improving relationships, attitudes and respect to address issues such as cultural inclusion, Māori education, parent involvement and integrating refugees. All of these efforts were aimed at improving the quality of teaching and learning, and student achievement.

Mark came to Victory School with a mandate to make changes to achieve these goals, and he believes he has had an impact on the quality of teaching in the school since he has been principal. "I think the culture of what is happening in the classrooms has changed to be more [curriculum] focused." His main concern for the school is pedagogy and quality teaching and learning. He believes this is about teachers having a philosophy of care and showing it in their actions, including students in their programmes and moving children forward in spite of their backgrounds.

Mark is proud and animated when discussing data and documentation that confirm the school's success in raising student achievement. Part of his vision for the school is that a systematic way of documenting school and student success should be developed to better demonstrate the difference the school is making to students' achievement. This is well underway. Mark used researchers from the Families Commission and 10 years of school data to construct tables to illustrate student achievement over 10 years, using the designations ABOVE, AT and BELOW in literacy, numeracy and writing. ESOL[3] students' data were not included. Students were placed in achievement categories based on teacher judgements, referred to as OJT (overall teacher judgement) in the national standards' literature. As a result, gut feelings have been converted into statistical data, thereby affirming the positive impact the school has had on its students. Furthermore, the trend data allow for the continual fine-tuning of systems and processes.

Conclusion

A number of key leadership themes are apparent in Mark's case study, including:
- the power of his vision for the school and community, and the way that vision has been accepted by children, adults and the community
- the absorbing story of how a community transformed as a result of change driven from within the school
- the integration of many ethnicities into the school and community
- the building of strong home–school and institutional partnerships
- an air of positivity in the school.

A common theme prevails: the exercise of moral leadership. The criteria advocated by Fullan (2001, 2003), Sergiovanni (1992), Greenfield (1999) and Starratt (2004) can be seen in all that Mark does in his school. He is regarded as a visionary, a driver of change, a relationship builder and a link between people. His leadership has its origins in the community, and this is underpinned by his effective use of strategic leadership and understanding of cultural change.

---

3   Students for whom English is a second language.

Although there is an impetus for school leadership to focus on pedagogical leadership (Robinson, Hohepa, and Lloyd, 2009), Mark's story demonstrates that we should give due consideration to other aspects of leadership, such as building community in order to achieve long-term, sustainable improvements in student learning. This study has revealed the importance of personal and cultural dimensions of school leadership, and the interrelatedness of the principal's values, beliefs and actions, and managing and leading behaviours.

Reflections for readers

Moral leadership

Moral leadership seems to best characterise the beliefs and actions of the principal in this study. According to Myatt (2007):

> Moral leadership is about doing the right things rather than doing things right. Doing the right things is a trait that causes leaders to be guided by their instincts, principles, values and desire to achieve. It is a leader's ability to do the right things that innovate, motivate, create and inspire. Doing the right thing is often times controversial, but true leaders are not daunted by the thought of conflict, as are most managers. Leaders guided by doing the right thing are willing to step up and make the big decisions that open markets, exploit opportunities, and drive innovation. (Myatt, 2007, p. 1)

Furman (2003) cites Sergiovanni (1992, p. 57), who argues that schools are "moral communities" requiring the development of a distinct leadership based in "moral authority." Similarly, Starratt (1998) argues that learning is intrinsically a moral activity, and that leadership within such an environment naturally and necessarily involves principals attending to the moral character of what the community is trying to do.

When leaders truly believe that their prime goal is the welfare of their followers, they get results (O'Toole, 1995). That is clear in Mark's case. Moral leadership is using one's attributes to improve people's lives. Leadership rooted in moral values starts with how people are treated, how they are shown respect, and how they are interacted with. It is not only fair and just; it is also highly effective in today's complex organisations. It also means helping people to agree on common values and goals. Schools cannot develop and grow if individuals within that school do not have common values and goals (Fullan, 2003). It is the leader's job to help people achieve that. Being a moral leader is also about empowering everyone in the organisation to be a leader and to achieve their goals.

There is no shortage of lists about what it means to be or to exercise moral leadership. For example, O'Toole (1995) sees moral leadership as being an integral part of who the person is or what they are. At a practical level, Bottery (1992) maintains that exercising moral leadership involves: promoting personal growth, treating people as ends in themselves, fostering rationality, viewing human beings as resourceful humans, creating an ethos where measures of democracy can be introduced and replicated, and appreciating the place of individuals as citizens.

Implications for action

Fullan (2003) concentrates on new directions and new contexts that require that individuals take personal action to clarify and strengthen their moral perspective and commitment. Individuals in organisations also need to ensure their organisation develops and practises a collective educational morality. Fullan identifies two implications for school leaders. The first is to take action consistent with the moral journey; the second is to push for and be responsible to system opportunities to deepen and extend moral purpose. One way to do this is for schools to participate in district-wide initiatives that advance the cause of schooling.

There is much we do not know about moral leadership. Greenfield (1999) believes this can be overcome by studying the social relations and the meanings and perspectives underlying what school leaders are doing in their social relations with others, and the reasons they give for their actions and the views they hold. By studying the basis of the commitments underlying a school leader's aims, we might obtain a clearer understanding of the emotional dimensions of being a school leader. In turn, we might be in a better position to help principals improve their moral leadership.

The following questions are put forward for readers' reflections:
- To what extent is your leadership based on moral purpose?
- Under what circumstances might moral leadership come into conflict with other forms of leadership?
- What is the connection between leading with moral purpose and shared leadership in pursuit of learning?
- What would change in your school or centre if moral leadership was given a greater emphasis?

Suggested further reading

Duignan, P. (2006). *Educational leadership: Key challenges and ethical tensions*. London, UK: Cambridge University Press.

Haydon, G. (2007). *Values for educational leadership*. London, UK: Sage.

O'Mahony, G. R., Barnett, B. G., & Matthews, R. J. (2006). *Building culture: A framework for school improvement*. Moorabbin, VIC: Hawker Brownlow Education.

Stoll, L. (2003). School culture and improvement. In M. Preddy, R. Glatter, & C. Wise (Eds.), *Strategic leadership and educational improvement* (pp. 93–108). London, UK: Open University / Paul Chapman.

Waitere-Ang, H., & Adams, P. (2005). Ethnicity and society. In P. Adams, R. Openshaw, & J. Hamer (Eds.). *Education and society in Aotearoa New Zealand* (pp. 101–125). Victoria: Thomson/Dunmore Press.

References

Bottery, M. (1992). *The ethics of educational management: Personal, social and political perspectives on school organization.* London: Cassell.

Fullan, M. (2001). *Leading in a culture of change.* San Francisco: Jossey-Bass.

Fullan, M. (2003). *The moral imperative of school leadership.* Thousand Oaks: Corwin Press.

Furman, G. C. (2003). Moral leadership and the ethic of community. *Values and Ethics in Educational Administration, 2*(1), 8.

Greenfield, W. D. (1999). *Moral leadership in schools: Fact or fancy?* Paper presented at the Annual Meeting of the American Educational Research Association, Monteal, Canada.

Myatt, M. (2007). *Leadership matters: The CEO survival manual: What it takes to reach the C-suite and stay there.* Retrieved from http://www.n2growth.com/blog/doing-the-right-thing/ 22 March 2011.

Notman, R. (2009). The softer skills of leadership: Stories and strategies of six successful New Zealand school principals. *Journal of Educational Leadership, Policy and Practice, 24*(1), 1-3.

O'Toole, J. (1995). *Leading change: The argument for values-based leadership.* New York: Ballantine Books.

Robinson, V., Hohepa, M., & Lloyd, C. (2009). *School leadership and student outcomes: Identifying what works and why - best evidence synthesis iteration [BES].* Wellington: Ministry of Education.

Sergiovanni, T. J. (1992). *Moral leadership: Getting to the heart of school improvement.* San Francisco: Jossey-Bass.

Starratt, R. J. (1998). Grounding moral educational leadership in the morality of teaching and learning. *Leading and Managing, 4*(4), 243-255.

Starratt, R. J. (2004). *Ethical leadership.* San Francisco: Jossey-Bass.

CHAPTER 11

Invitational Leadership: A School where Students Inhabit the Digital Space

Colin Dale and Richard Smith

Colin Dale
Principal, West Harbour School (1987)
Principal, Kaikohe West Primary School (1988–1990)
Deputy Principal and Principal, Gladstone Primary School (1990–2002)
Principal, Murrays Bay Intermediate (2002–present)

Introduction and background

The major leadership theme that characterises this case study is *invitational leadership*. This particular form of leadership best exemplifies Colin's style as a leader. The evidence of this style of leadership is demonstrated through his words, actions and the behaviours he exhibits. Colin is the principal of Murrays Bay Intermediate School, an invitational school where the staff and students are able to make visitors feel at ease in a modern digital environment. Students and staff are welcoming, and the school is well led by a capable and affable principal who has high standards for himself and those he leads. While most educational leaders have followers, Colin creates a democratic environment where others at all levels of the organisation feel empowered to take leadership initiative and model positive leadership behaviours. This extends to the student body as well as the teaching personnel.

This chapter is slightly different to others in this collection. It is presented as a dialogic and interactive narrative between the two participants. Colin and Richard worked in partnership to write the chapter, with Colin located in Auckland and

Richard in Singapore. Colin and Richard have been professional colleagues for about a decade and have interacted professionally in a number of areas. The process of co-writing involved Richard sending outlines of questions to Colin, who responded via email. Richard then fleshed the concepts out, added some of the references and edited where necessary, with Colin's permission. What follows reads like a blend between an interview and a narrative of Colin's vision for successful leadership and student learning. The questions have been included to structure the discussion.

Colin has been the principal of Murrays Bay Intermediate since 2002. The school is ranked decile 10 and serves the largely middle-class population of North Shore City in Auckland. The students are in their 7th and 8th years of schooling. In 2010 a total of 1,020 students were enrolled at the school, including 66 international students, most of whom came from Korea. Previously Colin had served as principal at two low-decile schools, West Harbour School in West Auckland and Kaikohe West Primary in the Far North (each for approximately 2 years). He was deputy principal at Kaikohe and then principal from 1988 to 1990. His longest-serving principalship was at Gladstone Primary in Mt Albert, for approximately 12 years (from 1990 to 2002). These formative experiences in leadership at other schools have allowed Colin to appreciate the differences in the organisational cultures of schools, which are determined by the environment in which they are set.

Arrival and position at the school

When Colin first arrived at Murrays Bay Intermediate he found a well-organised institution that boasted a fine reputation. Nonetheless, although the school had benefited from strong leadership under the previous principal, it was ready for the next step in its journey. The most pressing and obvious areas for development were in teaching and learning. In addition to continuing to lead a high-performing school, Colin's challenge was to create a vision that would take the school into the next phase of a changing future. His personal and professional philosophy is premised on the belief that people are the treasures of any place and need to be treated as such. It is the prospect of making a difference to all the people in his care that drives him as a leader.

Ongoing academic study and continuing professional development have informed Colin's leadership practice

Ongoing academic study and continuing professional development have informed Colin's leadership practice and helped him in supporting the school's journey towards becoming a more effective learning institution. He believes that a special privilege of being a leader in education has been the opportunities he has had to serve on many principal organisation committees, as well as being involved in Vision Schools.[1] This organisation comprised an innovative group of principals who wished to pursue different approaches to leadership, and who advocated for the maximum self-management environment politically possible. Colin has also enjoyed a number of scholarship awards, including a 6-month ASB Travelling Fellowship to study gifted and talented education in the United States, Canada and the United Kingdom, an inaugural fellowship with the Unitec Educational Management academic programme, and a Distinguished Educator award from the University of Auckland.

RS: What are the leadership theories, pedagogies and philosophies that you draw upon?

CD: More often than not, schools that are successful believe in something. This was confirmed to me in 1993 when I visited numerous schools over a 6-month period in the USA, UK and Canada. It was very apparent that the most successful schools had a philosophy or understanding that underpinned their organisational behaviour. Accordingly, my very first strategic task on arriving at Murrays Bay Intermediate was to engage the staff in coming to an understanding of what the school "believes" as an organisation. They identified the informed teaching practices and understandings they thought the school should value and promote as an organisation. The staff decided that it would be best to draw on a detailed understanding of particular well-known educational theories. For instance, it was decided that Murrays Bay Intermediate would be an *invitational school* (Novak, 1992), a school that understood the age group the staff were privileged to be teaching and one that used programmes that were so dynamic and interesting that the young people would literally *run* to school!

The first step in implementing this understanding was to remove potential barriers to the students' involvement in school life. For example, the use of photocopiers was extended to students free of charge, with colour printing also allowed. We allowed the students to use cell phones at school, including their camera, calculator and other interesting functions. In the process, the school became completely digital and was no longer centred around desks or the teacher at the front of the classroom. I was fully aware that the students at Murrays Bay Intermediate were highly motivated digital "natives" (see Prensky, 2001), so we began to utilise podcasting and other contemporary technologies to enhance sharing outcomes. We also encouraged programmes that were authentic for each person and allowed personalised goals and ownership to shape students' learning experiences.

---

1 Vision Schools was established in the early 1990s as the Bulk-Funded Schools Association. It was dissolved in 2008 when the National coalition government came to power.

The theoretical basis for these changes noted above was Lorin Anderson and David Krathwohl's "revised Bloom's taxonomy" (Anderson and Sosniak, 1994; Anderson and Krathwohl, 2001) and Howard Gardner's (1999, 2006) idea of "multiple intelligences." These were used in conjunction with the teaching and use of emotional intelligence. On a more practical side, we introduced a high-performance sports programme to complement the school's extensive music, dance and graphic arts programmes to allow students to make their life choices at an early age.

After these ideas were embedded and accepted by every member of the school, we spent energy developing a tool for measuring and enhancing teachers' abilities in the art of teaching, using research on effective pedagogy. First we introduced a leadership coaching development programme to support the distributed leadership that had developed in the school over the years. We then established a teacher coaching programme using a matrix of researched principles of effective teaching as a resource for measuring each individual teacher's pedagogy. This matrix comprises six measureable dimensions of building learning-focused relationships, learning understandings, assessment literacy, promoting further learning (which includes deeper learning), active reflections, and 21st century learning.

We spent energy developing a tool for measuring and enhancing teachers' abilities in the art of teaching, using research on effective pedagogy

Description of the school

Although many of its students achieve extraordinarily well academically, Murrays Bay Intermediate attracts a greater than usual number of students who have special educational and social needs. This is because the school's reputation has been enhanced by the personalisation of specific programmes planned for each student, including the move towards a more digital approach that is appealing and engaging to the learner. Families are positive towards and supportive of the school. We keep in regular contact with parents and caregivers using a software programme called *School Links*, which uses texts and emails to inform families about what is going on at the school. The school website can be translated into the six languages used by families at our school by a simple click of a button. In addition, an intranet facility called *KnowledgeNet* allows families to access the school's planning, classroom programmes, assessment information, daily television broadcast, homework, newsletters and individual class information.

RS: How would you describe the ethos of the school?

CD: Continually developing. One recent development in ethos has been the alignment of the school's teaching philosophy with the four important Māori aspirations of:
- manaakitanga —we will teach and lead with moral purpose
- pono—we will help our people to have self-belief
- ako—we will empower our people to be lifelong learners
- āwhinatanga—all our people will be guided and supported as they will guide and support others (Ministry of Education, 2008).

By adopting the essence of these Māori achievement strategies, which are designed to help overcome failure in learning, we are now able to boast success for all students.

RS: In what ways is Murrays Bay Intermediate a happy place for students and teachers?

CD: Ongoing surveys report that staff and students are genuinely happy at school. The number of opportunities the staff have to contribute to the character of the school and their empowering and dynamic attitude have led to the development of a school that is focused on people, not systems. Being an *invitational school* means that we have *expectations* rather than *rules*. School should be an enjoyable place—it belongs to us all!

> *Being an invitational school means that we have expectations rather than rules*

Leadership issues and challenges

Leadership at Murrays Bay Intermediate is designed around professional ideals such as inquiry, pedagogy, performance and development, coaching, self-review and community liaison. The democratic team approach to school leadership relies on respectful positive relationships among all adults and students. Professional, high-level conversations permeate the school.

The school has developed and transformed so much in recent years it would have been difficult for the leadership tasks not to have changed. The leadership capacity of the staff has been extended and real strategic leadership positions have been created that involve trusting people to deliver important tasks. These include a range of directorship roles for senior staff, such as a community liaison role, a director of development and performance, a director of pedagogy, a manager of information, a director of research and inquiry, a director of coaching, and a director of international relations, separate from the director of international students.

Reasons for choosing a leadership role

RS: What motivated you to become an educational leader?

CD: I really wanted to do leadership differently. The lack of empathy for creative difference and the uncritical, compliant group of people who foster government policy aggravated me. The most difficult task I have encountered has been dealing with the level of bureaucracy in education. The Ministry of Education, New Zealand Teachers Council and Education Review Office have shown very little understanding of the differences of a 21st century school. The constant audits are now becoming unreasonable. Where were the students in all of this? I have genuinely wanted to make a difference, to move from a mundane regulatory leadership model to a dynamic, inspiring, encouraging, creative, contemporary model of leading. Early on I wanted to learn from my tertiary colleagues who, in the field of educational management and leadership, offered courses that covered theories that made sense and were inherently powerful if developed in the right context. I drew on the reference works of Michael Fullan (1997, 2007) on change management and Carol Cardno's (1999, 2001, 2007) dilemma management work. These writings were particularly valuable in increasing my effectiveness in the workplace as a leader.

To move from a mundane regulatory leadership model to a dynamic, inspiring, encouraging, creative, contemporary model of leading

RS: What does being a principal leader mean to you?

CD: Leadership, in my view, is not about power. It is about influence. Being ambitious for others and supporting their ongoing leadership development benefits the organisation as a whole by harnessing these human resources and talents for the benefit of the students and other stakeholders in the school. Being a principal is a responsibility which, when exercised with integrity, can inspire and make a genuine difference to people's lives.

Successful leadership strategies

RS: What have been your most important successes in this school?

CD: The idea that a school serves its people carries with it the expectation that the people will be served well. If they are to be served well, then there is a need for us, as leaders, to make sure that what we are organising is relevant to their life growth as people. The skills the students learn at school need to be contemporary, and there needs to be a powerful, engaging balance between the socio-political reality of the "now" and the students' learning needs for the future. Moreover, the learning has to be sufficiently relevant and deep to change the knowledge paradigms of each child so that they are able to cope with future challenges.

All our developments, we felt, have to be empowering. They need to engage with contexts that are relevant for students and enable each student to develop the skills to transform learning into practice. This ideal is for all stakeholders in the school. Staff should, and do, feel valued, respected and inspired. For this to happen, it was important for us to budget for a huge increase in the professional development of staff. This is in line with Robinson, Hohepa and Lloyd's (2009) finding that teacher professional development has the greatest effect size (0.84) on student learning.

And there needs to be a powerful, engaging balance between the socio-political reality of the "now" and the students' learning needs for the future

An important leadership strategy for us was never to mandate responsibility. We found that when people chose to be part of an initiative, it was more acceptable because they wanted to be part of it, and this sense of personal ownership transferred to others involved. The most powerful strategy in developing our school culture was to allow people time to own the possibilities we were keen on developing. By giving people the opportunity to experience in detail what the vision was about by observing others, we found the buy-in was seamless and that no coercion or direction was necessary. The embedding of a school ideology and organisational culture takes time. To practise what will always be done means that it has to be done for some time before it is labelled "culture" in the school setting.

RS: Why have you gone in any particular direction(s)?
CD: We have chosen to develop the school around the idea that "school should not be as it was for our parents." In a rapidly changing world where knowledge is growing faster than in any other time in history, and where innovation and technology are transformed in what appears to be a 3-yearly cycle, we cannot afford as educators to ignore the future in which our students are going to work. We know that many of the jobs that are emerging are science- and/or technology-based and that a high percentage are not yet jobs that we know about. Therefore, we need to train our students to be able to cope in an environment that has change as a daily life skill.

RS: How have you gone about planning and implementing the change in the school culture?
CD: The planning for the change has been an ongoing process. We started with a vision that emanated from consultation with staff, students and the community.

Focus groups enabled me to outline some ideas as a starting point. I tabled a document and gave a presentation to each group on the changing world, globalisation and the effects they are having on our future. People engaged with enthusiasm and responded with passion, urging us to develop a contemporary school that is different from other schools on the North Shore. We had separate meetings with members of Māori and Asian communities to ascertain their perspectives, with interpreters to help with understanding if needed. This gave me a mandate to publish, for consultation, a strategic plan, which is updated every 3 years. It is on the school's web page as a blog. A survey of all four stakeholder groups—staff, students, community and board of trustees—enabled us to identify any perceptual gaps that gave rise to differences of opinion among stakeholder groups. This information allowed us to determine which aspects of their opinions needed more time and effort to develop.

The changes were, of course, transformational. The very fabric of the school was altered. The infrastructure had to be redesigned and a new organisational structure created. We created mini-schools with at least eight classes in each. These included learning potential (once called "special needs"), developing talents (once called "gifted and talented"), technology, visual arts, sports and recreation, and teacher development (recently changed to "performance and development"). Each mini-school has a director who is responsible and accountable for their area of school activity.

RS: What is your vision for the school?

CD: Our vision for the school is to provide learning that is invitational, relevant and transferable for students who are entering a world that is so dynamic and so innovative that we are unlikely to be able to truly understand what their needs might be in 10 or 15 years' time. Globalisation is a reality, where jobs are transferable from one side of the world to the other, and consumers can look across the world for the best products available, so high-order skills are at a premium. We owe it to our students that they are able to be among the finest!

Globalisation is a reality, where jobs are transferable from one side of the world to the other

The vision is to be a contemporary school which uses the very best in research and understanding so as to be continually informed about best practice, pedagogically and in curriculum delivery. The personalisation of learning that complements our vision to be an organisation goes beyond the usual "we treat everyone as equal and encourage each student to reach their potential." We genuinely value and promote uniqueness, individuality, multi-ethnic understanding, and teachers' abilities to find individual ways of reaching our students in their middle years.

RS: What changes/new directions are you planning to bring about over the next 2 years?

CD: We plan to work on making the school environment less institutional. New gardens, a new auditorium with walls that constantly change colour, student cafés, and meeting places will all contribute to a more *invitational* space for students. We also plan to make the role of the students' voice in their school more effective. Students will be able to attend executive meetings and contribute more informed information about their school. The students have recently formed an action council and we will now train them to talk more about their learning. Howard Gardner (1999) proposes that students can and should know everything about their learning and ways of learning. In line with this, we intend to share what we know about leadership with those who are being led.

The increasing importance of global perspectives will be an ongoing focus of development. For example, we plan to redesign our social studies curriculum, which we will call global perspectives, to include constructs that embrace global concerns on a wider level of understanding (for example, financial literacy).

Personal assessment of success

The major contribution I have made to the life of Murrays Bay Intermediate has been to make things possible. Providing the framework for a visionary approach that is empowering for all who are a part of the school community has made a significant difference. Creating positivity through using a team approach, where everyone shares in the successes of change, has been a hallmark of the ethos of the school. I have been able to share a vision that has captured the interest of everyone, which, in turn, has helped them to accept and add to the dream in positive, constructive ways.

RS: What brings you the most professional satisfaction from the job?

CD: The most satisfaction comes from the reality that the changes that have characterised Murrays Bay Intermediate have been sustained beyond the transformational stage. It has been terrific to observe the embedding of the changes so that the next new stages can be implemented and the organisational culture improved incrementally. For example, all classes now learn using an inquiry approach that relies on the idea of "feed forward." Each student has their own research question on a rich, fertile issue, which is shared in a seminar fashion with their peers. The seminars rely on presentations that are innovative and rely on the many wonderful technological possibilities for presentation.

This means the students experience a wide range of knowledge and learning, instead of the traditional subject-based approach, where the class would learn about one class-centred topic (for example, the Bedouins). This approach answers some of the challenges of 21st century learning, especially in regard to the constant flow of new knowledge and information that young people face with the global knowledge explosion. Students now take responsibility for their own learning through developing an understanding of their learning intentions and how those intentions would translate and look if the students successfully completed the programme outcomes.

Students now take responsibility for their own learning through developing an understanding of their learning intentions

The more difficult aspects of the job

RS: What do you see as the key challenges in your leadership role?
CD: The challenges in my leadership role are many and varied. Because the vision for the school is steeped in theoretical research it is difficult to share the rich, complex understanding with the community, especially when there is a 50 percent turn-over of students and parents every year (an intermediate school has Years 7 and 8 students only). The efforts to "reach and teach" the community have been undermined by the fact that so few people attend the forums that are held each term. People are busy, and this is not a priority for them.

The ability to find time in the busy schedule of a school has been challenging. We introduced a television programme coordinated by the students, which is broadcast every day for all stakeholders between 8.45 and 9.00 am. The programme covers all the school's administrative issues and notices, provides advertisements for activities and is a forum for sharing student performances and successes. An effect of this initiative is that meetings are not over-burdened with administration. Instead, priority can now be given to teaching and learning, and we do not need to create extra time to meet organisational goals.

Conclusion

It is clear from Colin's responses and the vignettes he provides that he is a visionary leader who can empower others—staff and students alike. The school models a 21st century learning environment and compares favourably to the technologically rich schools in other countries such as Singapore. Colin uses modern pedagogical strategies and research-informed evidence to lead a highly dedicated and dynamic professional staff. The success of Colin's leadership is reflected in the school's

Education Review Office evaluation reports. As a leader who wishes to promote his educational community nationally and on an international scale, Colin welcomes visitors to the school, including international delegations of overseas educators. He is always keen to showcase Murrays Bay Intermediate as a 21st century educational enterprise that is truly invitational.

Reflections for readers

The dialogue between Colin and me as educators has led to ongoing discussions on leadership. Several themes were prominent, and we invite readers to reflect on these and to ponder the questions we raise. The major themes were: Colin's leadership styles, the major theorists and educational theories that inspire him, how he encourages and promotes leadership throughout the school, the influences he thinks are not as positive for education, and the ways in which he intends to lead the school in future.

We leave readers to consider the following reflective questions:
- Are there ways in which Colin's values of leadership are reflected in your own educational organisation?
- In what ways are your own organisation's invitational spaces available for all your stakeholders? Could your place of work be described as invitational?
- What types of leadership theories are drawn upon where you work?
- Do the leaders of your organisation use theories from outside of mainstream education to inform their educational philosophy?
- In what ways can you envision a different future for leaders in education through the enhanced use of ICT tools?
- In what ways is the culture of the organisation shaped by the vision of its leadership and wider community?
- What have you learnt about leadership, leadership capacity-building and succession planning through reading this chapter?

Suggested further reading

Purkey, W., & Novak, J. (1988). *Education: By invitation only*. Bloomington, IN: Phi Delta Kappan Educational Foundation.
Purkey, W., & Novak, J. (1996). *Inviting school success: A self concept approach to teaching, learning, and democratic process* (3rd ed.). Belmont, CA: Wadsworth.
Robinson, V. (2008). Forging the links between distributed leadership and student outcomes. *Journal of Educational Administration, 46*(2), 241–256.
Robinson, V., Lloyd, C., & Rowe, K. (2008). The impact of leadership on student outcomes. *Educational Administration Quarterly, 44*(5), 635–674.

References

Anderson, L., & Krathwohl, D. (Eds.). (2001). *A taxonomy for learning, teaching, and assessing: A revision of Bloom's taxonomy of educational objectives.* New York, NY: Longman.

Anderson, L., & Sosniak, L. (1994). *Bloom's taxonomy: A forty-year retrospective.* Chicago, IL: National Society for the Study of Education.

Cardno, C. (1999). Problem-based methodology in leadership development: Interventions to improve dilemma management. *New Zealand Journal of Educational Administration, 14,* 44–51.

Cardno, C. (2001). Managing dilemmas in appraising performance: An approach for school leaders. In D. Middlewood & C. Cardno (Eds.), *Managing teacher appraisal and performance: A comparative approach* (pp. 143–159). London, UK: RoutledgeFalmer.

Cardno, C. (2007). Leadership learning: The praxis of dilemma management. *International Studies in Educational Administration, 35*(2), 33–50.

Fullan, M. (1997). *The new meaning of educational change* (2nd ed.). New York, NY: Teachers College Press.

Fullan, M. (2007). *The new meaning of educational change* (4th ed.). New York, NY: Teachers College Press.

Gardner, H. (1999). *Intelligence reframed: Multiple intelligences for the 21st century: The theory in practice.* New York, NY: Basic Books.

Gardner, H. (2006). *Multiple intelligences: New horizons in theory and practice.* New York, NY: Basic Books.

Ministry of Education. (2008). *Kiwi leadership for principals: Informing principals' professional learning.* Wellington, NZ: Author.

Novak, J. (1992). *Advancing invitational thinking.* San Francisco, CA: Caddo Gap Press.

Prensky, M. (2001). Digital natives, digital immigrants. *On the Horizon, 9*(5), 1–6.

Robinson, V., Hohepa, M., & Lloyd, C. (2009). *School leadership and student outcomes: Identifying what works and why: Best evidence synthesis iteration.* Wellington: Ministry of Education.

CHAPTER 12

Building Leadership Success in a New Zealand Education Context

Ross Notman

Introduction

In line with the overall directions of the ISSPP project, these New Zealand case studies of successful educational leadership seek to provide contextualised answers to two major research questions:
- What practices do successful leaders use?
- What gives rise to successful educational leadership?

This discussion chapter will synthesise these New Zealand case study findings by using Donaldson's (2008) core leadership knowledge areas as an organising framework. The findings will be compared to the international literature on educational leadership and will be grouped according to the following thematic headings:
- pedagogical leadership (what is effective learning?)
- professional leadership (what makes a school or early childhood centre effective as an organisation?)
- interpersonal leadership (how do leaders cultivate robust working relationships with and among others?)
- intrapersonal leadership (what beliefs and values guide the work of a leader?; do they understand themselves well enough to choose wisely how they will act as a leader?).

I will examine how leaders maintain their success over time, and will summarise some of the challenges and tensions even a successful leader faces in the course of their daily work. The discussion concludes with suggestions for re-conceptualising the role of educational leader in a democratic climate, which calls for leaders' simultaneous attention to constituent demands for increased participation and accountability, and to broader external spheres of influence and need.

Pedagogical leadership

It is clear from these principal case studies that successful leadership is based on the core business of teaching and learning. Leaders have a vision of teaching and learning that aims to increase levels of student achievement. They see possibilities and creative opportunities, rather than limitations, in the early childhood curriculum (Ministry of Education, 1996) and school curriculum (Ministry of Education, 2007). Leaders encourage collaboration among their staff through stimulating learning conversations in which teachers make meaning together to gain new insights and knowledge that, in turn, lead to changed pedagogical practices (Stoll, 2010). Case study leaders also encourage the explicit sharing of teaching and learning strategies, and pay close attention to accurate student assessment data to help identify the learning and skill development needs of individual students.

Of particular interest in the early childhood and primary school studies is a focus on building school–parent partnerships that will support children's learning. In the case of Southbridge School, Peter Verstappen advocates the active engagement of parents in ongoing dialogues about learning through focus group discussions, and through teaching and learning messages in the form of a weekly school newsletter. He advances the concept of a "vanishing" school, whereby "school, home and community will cease to be mutually exclusive learning environments in the minds of children" (Chapter 2, p. 18). Similarly, influential connections are made between teachers and whānau in the early childhood study of Te Kōpae Piripono. Staff believe it is important to engage with families about expectations and contributions to their child's learning, build open and honest communication links with parents, value parental contribution and, as a consequence, promote a sense of belonging. Such school–family connections may also have a social justice outcome, as evidenced by Mark Brown's effective integration of immigrant families into Victory School and its community, which enables immigrant children to participate in the curriculum.

Leithwood, Jacobson and Ylimaki (2011) suggest reasons why such an emphasis on teaching and learning, together with instructional leadership, has occurred worldwide:

> A convergence of neo-liberal discourses that link economic prosperity to education and neo-conservative tendencies toward back-to-basics, subject-oriented teaching

and regular testing regimes may help to explain why so many principals in systems internationally have been influenced to place instructional practices at the very center of their work ... Collectively, the ISSPP research teams found that schools in every country studied were currently operating under greater accountability and public scrutiny than at any other time in the recent past. (pp. 19–20)

As noted, this pivotal focus on teaching and learning is replicated in international educational leadership research investigations of successful principals. For example, in Ylimaki's (2007) ISSPP study of instructional leadership approaches in four high-poverty, culturally diverse US schools, she found that successful leadership[1] was related, among other factors, to the principals' strong pedagogical knowledge and capacity-building skills. In national and international educational contexts, findings from Robinson, Hohepa and Lloyd's (2009) best evidence synthesis underline the crucial role of educational leadership in that "the closer educational leaders get to the core business of teaching and learning, the more likely they are to have a positive impact on students" (p. 47). Within New Zealand educational settings Robinson et al. identify educational leaders' capacity for creating educationally powerful connections with family, whānau and communities, and argue that these school–home connections can have a significant impact on improving student learning outcomes. Their meta-analysis also suggested to them that "where schools do not provide such leadership, business-as-usual may actually do educational harm (as, for example, when parents try to help with homework and inadvertently undermine achievement)" (p. 150).

Professional leadership

Successful educational leaders in this New Zealand study are characterised by their use of a range of common leadership strategies. These include adherence to a particular vision and philosophy; cultural changes; employment and motivation of quality teaching staff; building individual capability among staff through distributed leadership practices; and an acute contextual awareness, which results in a strong sense of advocacy. I will now look at each of these in turn.

Vision and philosophy

All of these leaders subscribe to an overarching vision for their school or centre. This confirms the importance to successful institutions of an underlying philosophy that informs organisational behaviour, educational directions and what Colin Dale terms one's "professional ideals." In Mark Brown's case, for example, his educational direction setting includes an allied vision for the inclusion of the immigrant community into the school environment, where they can share a positive sense of belief in themselves as well as in their children's learning.

---

1 In the US, "success" is defined by student achievement.

For Mark and other case study principals, it is imperative for the leader to articulate and communicate this vision effectively, both inside and outside the school. It is, as Kouzes and Posner (2007) suggest, a matter of "breathing life into your vision" (p. 154). Successful leaders also strive to project their vision into the future, not only on behalf of their organisation but, more importantly, for their students. As Colin Dale describes it, his school's vision has been to provide learning that is "invitational, relevant and transferable for students who are entering a world that is so dynamic and innovative that we are unlikely to be able to truly understand what their needs might be in 10 or 15 years' time" (Chapter 11, p. 130).

This key leadership strategy of vision building and implementation has been replicated in the international research literature. For example, one of the key themes identified in Duignan and Gurr's (2007) Australian studies of successful leaders is a clearly articulated philosophy, accompanied by a deep moral purpose. Ultimately, this philosophy aims to help students in their personal and learning development, and to reach for a better future. Like their New Zealand counterparts, successful Australian school leaders want to make a difference for their students.

Cultural changes

A number of successful leadership strategies revolve around the concept of cultural change for both students and staff. Leaders employ this type of strategy across different operational levels of their institution. First, there is the example of Victory School, where Mark Brown has used a culturally responsive style of leadership to address changes in ethnicity from a predominantly European student population to one that has significant numbers of immigrant and Māori children. Second, principals have overcome a negative learning culture by seeking and achieving improvements in academic performance, and by extending the arena of student learning to include co-curricular activities outside the classroom. A third cultural area with a student focus is the promotion of a culture built on an ethic of care. This is exemplified in Richard Inder's school, where a positive organisational culture portrays "a world that is exciting for the students and holds a future for them" (Chapter 6, p. 66).

This ethic of care also extends to enhancing a staff culture. In Richard Inder's case, this involves building staff confidence, teaching skills and morale, and enabling staff to move on from instances of emotional fragility caused by past events in the school. Some of the strategies involved changing the name, and hence the identity, of the school, employing new quality teachers, and promoting a shared values system among the staff. Jann Carvell at Fairhaven School assumed leadership of a special needs school in which there were few positive elements in the school culture, and deep-level systemic change was required at all operating levels: management, health, safety and governance. In Jann's case, systemic success has been brought about by, in part, her and the staff assuming budgetary control and clarifying decision-making systems within the school. Similar changes in organisational structures and management systems have taken place in other schools to accommodate and increase student learning potential and teacher professional development. These examples demonstrate a fundamental need for effective management systems in a successful school or centre, and serve to emphasise that the functions of leadership and management can be viewed as "a duality and not a dilemma" (Southworth, 2002, p. 7).

The New Zealand findings in relation to culturally diverse change are supported by findings in other ISSPP countries. In a study of successful leadership in two multi-ethnic Norwegian schools, Vedoy and Moller (2007) found that each principal played a pivotal role in working for democratic schooling, and that an ethic of care was crucial through focusing on possibilities and respect rather than on deficits. Similarly, Hoog and Johansson's (2005) Swedish study of three successful principals concluded that the leaders worked hard to enhance both academic knowledge and social goals, but also worked in alignment with the ideology and culture of the school district. In the USA, Johnson (2007) found that the success of three female principals was, among other factors, attributable to establishing culturally responsive and empowering relationships with diverse parent groups and members of the wider community. These cross-country findings have prompted Leithwood et al. (2011) to talk about the concept of "culturally sensitive leadership" and to conclude that this movement in the leadership field is

> a specific reflection of the more general understanding that all leaders work in contexts that are, in some measure, unique and that to be successful, leaders need to enact their practices in ways that are sensitive to those contexts. (p. 23)

Quality teaching

The recruitment and retention of quality teaching staff is a major leadership strategy (Day et al., 2009). Leaders see the importance of selecting teachers who are supportive of students' learning needs within a unique school context, and who are sympathetic to the school's values system and direction setting. When necessary, principals are prepared to spend time grounding new staff through a cultural induction process.

Clear expectations of teacher performance are laid down, especially when leaders wish to raise levels of student academic achievement. This was the case for Larry Ching. For him it meant raising staff expectations of student performance, which, in turn, led to a changed learning culture within the school. Across the leaders' case studies it appears that these expectations are combined with the promotion of educational goals, interpersonal relationships and clarity about the organisational culture. Underpinning these expectations is the ability of leaders to motivate staff to buy in to changes in teaching and learning, and to allow time for staff to "own" broad-based changes in the institution's ideology and organisational culture. Duignan and Gurr (2007) identified similar characteristics in Australian school leaders, in that they had an expectation of high professional standards for themselves and for their teachers, and were focused on creating a collaborative, collegial and inclusive school culture.

Distributed leadership

The educational leaders in these case studies work hard to build individual capacity in their teachers. This is achieved through professional development and, in particular, through their use of distributed leadership practices, in which "a larger number of people are involved in the work of others, are trusted with information, are involved in decision making, are exposed to new ideas and are participating in knowledge creation and transfer" (Harris, 2005, p. 165). Leaders see the strength of collective input within a professional community. They are prepared to change from traditional features of vertical leadership to structures in which roles and responsibilities are more widely distributed among staff, together with the requisite power and authority to carry out the responsibility. This applies not only to individual teachers but also to clusters of teams formed for specific purposes, such as futures planning, management oversight, programme review and extra-curricular activities. Richard Newton exemplifies this feature through his use of teams to share power: he provides the opportunity to lead, and to develop a climate of mutual trust and cooperation. In the early childhood case study, distributed leadership was broadened to include children, teachers and parents as a way to address inequitable power relationships.

However, even for successful educational leaders there are challenges in such collaborative activity. The concept of distributed leadership assumes that teachers will have the capability and skills, motivation and time to take up leadership responsibility. Small school or centre size, high staff turnover or the absence of experienced teachers may work against effective leadership distribution. Mike Sutton's case study acknowledges the vulnerability of distributing leadership among staff, whereby delegated tasks may not be carried out effectively, leading to project failure. This implies a need for leaders to distribute tasks in conjunction with clear goals and expected outcomes, and with appropriate support mechanisms in place.

The ISSPP literature reinforces the concept of capacity building as a leadership success factor (Giles, 2007; Leithwood et al., 2011). In a UK study of a successful primary principal, Day (2007) found that distributing leadership was one of the strategies used to encourage teacher ownership of school improvement measures. This mechanism for shared ownership delivered two messages: "First, it communicated a belief that many people, rather than one, are able to take responsibility for leading change. Second, it demonstrated the confidence and trust of the headteacher" (Day, 2007, p. 44).

Contextual awareness

Educational leadership does not operate in pedagogic isolation (Leithwood et al., 2010). It is subject to the pervasive influence of the school or centre context, and how that influence affects one's capacity to lead. Some of the case studies underline the importance of contextual awareness on the part of leaders. Mike Sutton's case emphasises the need for a new principal to take stock of the existing school context before embarking on change processes. Taking a broader view of contextual awareness, there is a geo-political and multigenerational context that Georgina Kingi finds herself in at St Joseph's. Not only is Georgina located in her Māori whakapapa (ancestry) but also by culture, ethnicity, political climate, time and space.

Allied to this contextual awareness is an accompanying advocacy role played by leaders on behalf of their students and wider school community. For example, Georgina Kingi clearly advocates on behalf of her female students in the face of negative stereotypes of the girls' capabilities, while Mark Brown and Jann Carvell are advocates for social justice in their inclusiveness of ethnic groups and of special needs students and their families, respectively. The combination of contextual awareness and advocacy can be central to the successful situational leadership practices New Zealand leaders use in their response to unique sets of educational circumstances (Notman & Henry, in press).

Interpersonal leadership

In a New Zealand self-managing schools environment, educational leaders have multiple accountabilities, in the form of students, staff, parents/caregivers, boards of trustees and educational agencies, including the Education Review Office (which undertakes school reviews) and the Ministry of Education (which sets national educational policy). Within this complex mix of personal and professional interconnections, successful leaders take care to model and build respectful, ongoing relationships with various school-related constituents. Georgina Kingi refers to this as "purposeful relations of interdependence" (Chapter 3, p. 29). She also draws a careful distinction between an interpersonal student–teacher relationship that seeks to enhance student self-esteem, and a professional learning relationship that seeks to improve a student's competencies and skills.

Like other leaders, Mike Sutton's case offers further instances of positive interpersonal relationship strategies. These include modelling leadership practice that incorporates visible elements of risk taking, as evidenced by sharing authority in distributing leadership roles among the staff; coaching activity for staff that links professional learning to classroom teaching; and a leadership presence through classroom interactions with teachers, resulting in a professional credibility that cements his status as a leader of learning.

These educational leaders strongly favour people-centred leadership. They demonstrate empathy, loyalty to school and community, a sensitively expressed ethic of care, and a lack of ostentation. The personal and professional integrity of the leaders is acknowledged by those with whom they work closely. This is a factor in gaining and maintaining the trust of others (Notman & Henry, 2009). The strategy of building trusting relationships is explicit in the case of Mike Sutton: "The process of building trusting relationships requires the leader to be vulnerable at times, 'to admit when you don't know', and to seek advice and support" (Chapter 4, p. 43). It is also evident in the case of Te Kōpae Piripono, where it was necessary to build reciprocal trust with parents who had entrusted their children's care and learning to early childhood staff.

Relational connectedness and trust building permeates these leadership case studies. The concept of emotional intelligence (Goleman, Boyatzis, & McKee, 2002) is critical to the success of these New Zealand leaders. They have an ability to "read" people and understand the impact of working alongside them instead of forcing an accommodation to fit their preferred way of working. It would appear that successful educational leaders develop relationships as a priority, and secure trust at a deeper level when the authenticity of their values and belief systems intersects and resonates with others.

Intrapersonal leadership

Research interest in the impact of personal dimensions on successful principalship has grown in recent years (Beatty, 2005; Begley, 2006; Milstein & Henry, 2008; Notman, 2008). This is exemplified by preliminary findings from the ISSPP project, especially in multi-perspective research conducted in UK schools, that leadership success is due to a number of factors, including "strong core values and beliefs, an abiding sense of agency, identity, moral purpose, resilience, and trust" (Day, 2005, p. 273). The New Zealand case studies in this book reinforce the influence of core values and belief systems on leadership behaviours. Leaders model what they believe in and demonstrate strength of conviction in their decision-making practices. Like Jan Anderson, the principal of Otago Girls' High School in a separate

New Zealand ISSPP case study (Notman, in press), these school and centre leaders communicate their personal vision and values by direction, words and deeds. They are acknowledged by their staff as authentic leaders who derive their credibility from personal integrity and from living out their values in the workplace.

Critical self-reflection enables leaders to prioritise their educational objectives, particularly in relation to time spent leading teaching and learning. Some leaders have found that reflexivity is a core disposition that promotes reflection before and after decision-making processes or events. In Mike Sutton's case, he begins with a process of wondering, and poses himself a series of critical questions: "For example, if he had ignored the context and looked solely at the event, might he have strategised and facilitated the process in a different way? If he had applied different values, would the outcome have been different?" (Chapter 4, p. 42).

The personal characteristic of resiliency is also a factor consistent with earlier ISSPP findings (Day & Leithwood, 2007). All New Zealand case study leaders were identified as being resilient. In relation to Milstein and Henry's (2008) resiliency model, they believe in their ability to make a difference for students, and to establish positive interpersonal relationships. They engage in critical self-reflection about their leadership role and future directions. They have the "ability to bounce back from adversity, learn new skills, develop creative ways of coping, and become stronger" (Milstein & Henry, 2008, p. 7). The influence of personal dimensions on educational leadership is well summarised by Day et al. (2010). In a report on UK findings of a 3-year national research project on the impact of leadership on student learning outcomes, they make 10 strong claims about successful school leadership. Claim 3 identifies head teachers' values as a key component in their success:

> Our claim is that the most successful school leaders are open-minded and ready to learn from others. They are flexible rather than dogmatic within a system of core values. They are persistent in their high expectations of others, and they are emotionally resilient and optimistic. Such traits help explain why successful leaders facing daunting conditions are often able to push forward against the odds. Our research confirms this. (p. 7)

Sustaining leadership success

One of the interesting areas of the ISSPP project has been the exploration of factors underlying principals' ability to sustain leadership success over time. New Zealand case study leaders have been able to grow success in their schools and centres through the use of "layered leadership strategies" (Day et al., 2009, p. 200). In this instance, these layers include a focus on the teaching and learning process, support for staff professional development and for their own professional learning, collaborative leadership strategies and intrapersonal elements. I will now look at each of these in turn.

First, all the educational leaders support an ongoing emphasis on leading teaching and learning. They give priority to pedagogical matters over "administrivia", and are keen to address barriers to student learning and achievement. They aim to spend time in classrooms as a tacit symbol of their professional support for, and encouragement of, effective teaching and learning practices. In sustaining their pedagogical leadership, leaders can realise their ultimate goal, which is to make a difference to the lives of children through education and their holistic development.

Second, ongoing professional development provides both leaders and staff with opportunities to upskill and to maintain a strong learning base. Individual or cluster school involvement in national professional development contracts, quality learning circles, and professional learning group discussions based on up-to-date research are some examples of conduits through which leaders and teachers are exposed to new teaching and learning ideas. This continuation of professional learning aligns with Robinson et al.'s (2009) best evidence synthesis finding that leaders' promotion and participation in teacher learning and development has a significant effect on improving student learning outcomes. This is in addition to leaders' own personal and professional learning activities (such as formal university leadership study) and the mentoring of new principals to access the latest knowledge and trends in education.

Third, leaders maintain success through collaborative strategies of distributed leadership among the staff and shared decision making. At a macro level of educational management they are conscious of gaining buy-in from staff and boards of trustees to support their school's philosophy and direction setting. Several leaders also extend internal collaboration to include student input into relevant aspects of school life. In Colin Dale's school, for example, student "voice" is encouraged through their contribution to learning planning, while Larry Ching places great stock by senior student leadership training. These collaborative findings concur with others in the educational leadership literature (Harris & Muijs, 2005; Leithwood et al., 2010; Spillane, Healey, Parise, & Kenney, 2011). However, Timperley (2009) sounds a warning about the risks of distributing leadership over a larger group of people, thereby increasing the chances of a "greater distribution of incompetence" (p. 220). She suggests that expanding the distribution of leadership "is only desirable if the quality of the leadership activities contributes to assisting teachers to provide more effective instruction to their students" (p. 220).

Finally, intrapersonal leadership enables leaders to maintain an awareness of self in the job, and to take care of one's own physical and mental well-being as a self-management tool in sustaining success. A productive work–life balance and supportive family and friends are other key ingredients for sustaining resilience in the face of demanding leadership work. Leaders devote self-reflective time to evaluating their own leadership performance, as well as the staff teaching and student academic performance and attitudes to learning. It also appears that they take time to reflect on aspects of the personal self as well as the professional self, a dimension Gardner (1983) termed "intrapersonal intelligence": the ability to access and understand one's inner self and idiosyncratic personal emotions, feelings and aspirations.

Challenges and tensions

Successful educational leaders are not immune from experiencing a raft of challenges and tensions during the course of their work. Things that have an impact from the external educational environment include social and health issues of impoverished families, accompanied by pressures on the school or centre to become the hub or focal point of their community. Within educational workplaces, leaders face challenges such as upskilling staff for a digital age with which their students are already familiar, maintaining staff motivation in light of continuing social and educational change, and attending to the complexities of teachers' personal needs as well as their professional needs.

Tensions and dilemmas in relation to their students also have to be dealt with by successful leaders. These can take the form of planning new facilities to absorb student roll growth, working with behaviourally dysfunctional children, or weighing up the rights of the individual student to an education versus the common good of the majority of students to be taught in a stable learning environment. There are an increasing number of issues surrounding student safety from cyber bullying, and malevolent internet influences from social networking sites (Notman, 2009).

Re-conceptualising the role of educational leader

The job of a school or early childhood leader is not for the fainthearted. In an era of self-management in education it can be a stressful occupation "being accountable to everyone and being blamed for everything" (Crawford, Kydd, & Riches, 1997, p. 58). The job invariably involves a balancing act as the leader moves along a leadership/ management continuum, dealing with tensions and dilemmas caused by opposing forces. S/he may alternate between being democratic and exercising control, being critical and non-critical, confronting internal and external pressures, motivating staff to anticipate the future and offering them sufficient stability to cope with the present. Jirasinghe and Lyons (1996) reflected realistically that one is unlikely to find an educational leader fully capable of dealing with such a range of behaviours: "There is a danger that the specification sought would need an Archangel Gabriel to fulfil all of its requirements" (p. 88).

Not only are there challenges within the job, but leaders are also subjected to multiple role expectations from inside and outside their workplace. From a pragmatic viewpoint one cannot deny that the job of an educational leader is multidimensional. There can be few vocations where one is called on to perform the roles of sociologist, psychologist, community worker, politician, mediator, legal adviser, architect, building contractor, co-curricular coach, administrative manager and professional leader.

At a conceptual level, the role of the school principal has undergone fundamental change throughout the last century in response to social change and school reform movements. Beck and Murphy (1993) captured these changes in their metaphorical descriptions of progressive role expectations of the principal: values broker (1920s), scientific manager (1930s), democratic leader (1940s), theory-guided administrator (1950s), bureaucratic executive (1960s), humanistic facilitator (1970s) and instructional leader (1980s). To this listing could be added more recent New Zealand roles of technical administrator (1990s) and change manager (2000s). What metaphor would best describe the school leader's role in the decade beginning 2010?

Findings from the New Zealand case studies of successful leaders suggest that the scope of educational leadership is being expanded beyond atomised listings of professional standards, competencies and skills. The distinctive metaphors of previous decades are becoming blurred into an eclectic interpretation of leadership roles. First, the core role of *pedagogical leader* is rightly at the forefront of leadership practice, with its student-oriented focus on improving teaching and learning outcomes. Robinson et al.'s (2009) best evidence synthesis supports the crucial input of New Zealand school leaders in improving classroom pedagogy and student achievement and well-being. It underlines a pragmatic challenge in New Zealand schools in terms of how we adjust a self-managing school system to "ensure that we have sufficient effective leaders with the time and support they need" (p. 36).

Second, it is evident from these cases, and from the ISSPP literature, that *intrapersonal leadership* is an underlying factor in leaders' personal and professional growth. As Donaldson, Bowe, McKenzie and Marnik (2004) contend, the pursuit of self-knowledge and understanding by educational leaders should result in an enhanced "intrapersonal understanding of their 'platform' of belief about their work and, most important, about themselves as people and as leaders" (p. 540). This blend of personal and professional dimensions of educational leadership is advocated by West-Burnham (1997) in an earlier assessment of the dichotomy:

> There is no doubt that leaders need knowledge (or access to knowledge) and a range of skills in order to be effective. However, these have to be contextualised in terms of personal values, self-awareness, emotional and moral capability. This is not to produce another set of formulations but rather to argue for leaders who have self-knowledge and are able to learn and so grow personally. (p. 141)

However, it is within a third role function of professional leader that the metaphor may assume a different dimension for the next decade: that of the *contextually responsive leader*. Universal trends towards greater public participation in education (Woods, 2005) and the advent of self-managing schools in New Zealand have brought about increasing demands for the democratisation of leadership in the form of distributed leadership and shared decision making among staff; a greater impact of student voice in school life; and gaining community support for the school/centre's philosophy and direction setting. In addition, leaders have been called upon to take a responsive role with regard to external demands and influences, and to building trusting relationships with their extended community. This responsive role has been accentuated in New Zealand education by an expectation that leaders will meet multiple needs and be answerable to multiple accountability points within their educational constituencies; for example, the learning needs of students; the social, economic and cultural needs of families and ethnic groups, as they relate to well-being, financial hardship and diversity, respectively; the professional needs of teachers and boards of trustees; and the policy and regulatory requirements of educational agencies such as the Ministry of Education and the Education Review Office.

Bottery (2004) supports these considerations as they lead to a broader ecological view of educational leadership appropriate to a changing global context in which "dominant social functions are increasingly organised around networks, and in this 'network society' as Castells (1996) calls it, the new power is influence through integration and interdependence, rather than power over others" (Harris, 2008, p. 140). This networking trend, together with a momentum in seeking more democratic forms of leadership, explains the emphasis on devolving responsibility for leadership among individual teachers, teams or ad hoc groups. This re-direction of leadership control and power not only encourages participant ownership and commitment to a learning organisation, but also establishes a potential launching pad for knowledge creation and transfer.

This ecological approach to understanding the realities of the leadership role shows that educational leadership does not exist in a vacuum, but rather within a socio-cultural-economic-political context. This blended context can affect school/centre directions, and has the potential to both enhance and constrain one's capability to lead and to manage. In this way, an ecological view of educational leadership supports a contextually responsive role, as educational leaders react to and engage with different contextual layers of influence.[2]

---

2 Parallels can be made with Bronfenbrenner's (1979) ecological systems for understanding children's development, and with Goodlad's (2006) views of a healthy school, built on an ecological model of education that comprises "interactions, relationships and interdependences within a defined environment" (p. 90).

Educational unit "systems" can be delineated as the student, the family and extended school community, educational leaders (including teachers), educational agencies, and society in general. The educational leader is in an unenviable position, caught between the micro world of the student and their family/community and the macro world of educational agencies and society's educational expectations and values. Located in the middle of this ecological system, the educational leader is subject to overarching social, economic, cultural and political spheres of influence and need. This is outlined in the figure below.

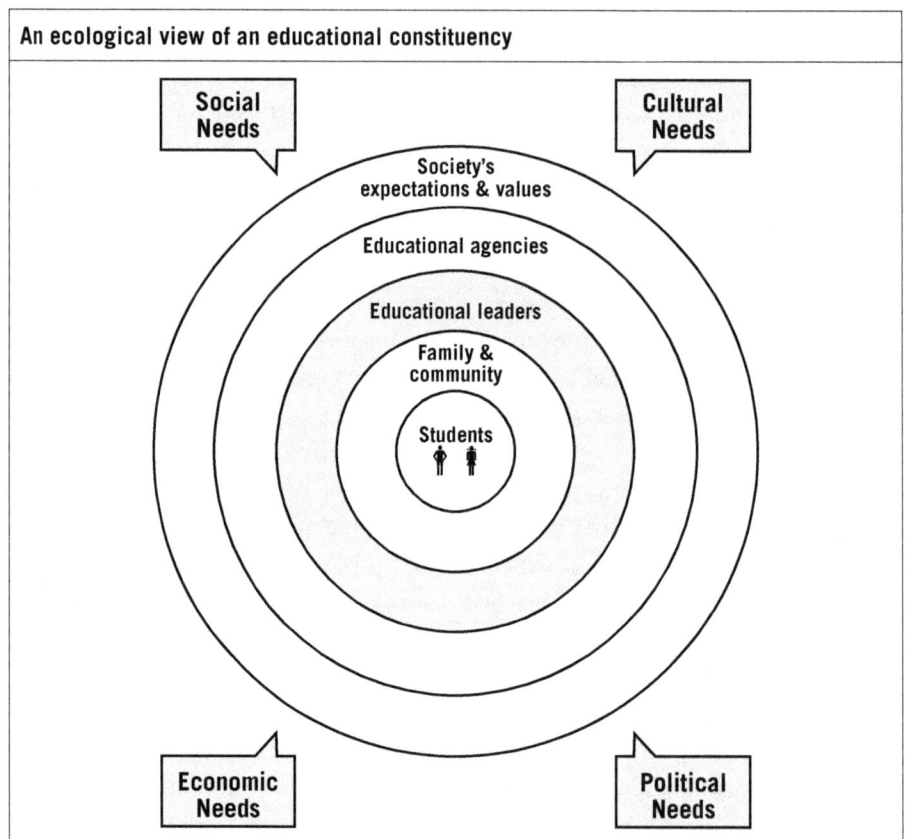

An ecological view of an educational constituency

Thus, the role of professional educational leader can be re-conceptualised as an integrated and interdependent mosaic of pedagogical, intrapersonal and contextually responsive leadership functions that are subject to other forces within and outside of each educational institution. Hargreaves (2011) describes this as "fusion leadership", which moves beyond traditional notions of technical competencies and skills:

Instead, it is the psychological integration of a personality and a community combined with the knowledge, empathy and strategic capability to know what parts of one's own and one's colleagues' leadership are the right ones, for the right time and for the challenges at that moment. Leadership beyond expectations is not a fission of competencies but a fusion of qualities and characteristics within oneself, one's community and over time. (p. 239)

Conclusion

This New Zealand research reveals meaningful insights from 10 case studies about the dedication and work of successful educational leaders in an early childhood centre, and intermediate, primary and secondary schools. The research findings, together with identical themes in the ISSPP literature, reinforce the complexity of the world of educational leadership across global settings, and reveal a paradoxical mix of control, compliance and responsiveness. There is an ever-present unpredictability about educational leadership in changing times which precludes giving an adequate description of the role within any one particular leadership model.

Hence, an eclectic approach has been used here that incorporates the pedagogical leadership of teachers and students, contextually responsive leadership that promotes the relational connectedness of leader with constituents, and an inner leadership of self where one's values, motivations and intrapersonal intelligence inform leadership behaviours. These multiple layers contribute to our understanding of the holistic enactment of leadership.

In light of this concept of educational leadership as a holistic endeavour, it is appropriate to conclude this chapter with the final two stanzas from Davison's poem. The words are particularly relevant to contemporary educational settings, where there is a need to understand an expanding concept of what it means to lead and what it means to be human:

> Not the time to ape or mirror wider culture
> Time to get back to a sense of community
> Reach across internal rifts
> Transcend disciplines
> Care deeply
> Earn trust.
>
> In moments of grace
> you bring people together
> in relationship vignettes
> where they appreciate
> and are in awe
> of each other.

(Davison & Burge, 2010, p. 129)

References

Beatty, B. (2005). Emotional leadership. In B. Davies (Ed.), *The essentials of school leadership* (pp. 122–144). London, UK: Paul Chapman Publishing & Corwin Press.

Beck, L. G., & Murphy, J. (1993). *Understanding the principalship: Metaphorical themes 1920s–1990s.* New York, NY: Teachers College Press.

Begley, P. T. (2006, October). *Self-knowledge, capacity and sensitivity: Prerequisites to authentic leadership by school principals.* Paper presented at Values-based Leadership Conference, Victoria, Canada.

Bottery, M. (2004). *The challenges of educational leadership.* London, UK: Paul Chapman Publishing.

Bronfenbrenner, U. (1979). *The ecology of human development.* Cambridge, MA: Harvard University Press.

Castells, M. (1996). *The information age: The rise of the networked society.* London, UK: Blackwell.

Crawford, M., Kydd, J., & Riches, C. (1997). *Leadership and teams in educational management.* Buckingham, UK: Open University Press.

Davison, P., & Burge, E. J. (2010). Between dissonance and grace: The experience of post-secondary leaders. *International Journal of Lifelong Education, 29*(1), 111–131.

Day, C. (2005). Principals who sustain success: Making a difference in schools in challenging circumstances. *International Journal of Leadership in Education, 8*(4), 273–290.

Day, C. (2007). Sustaining the turnaround: What capacity building means in practice. *International Studies in Educational Administration, 35*(3), 39–48.

Day, C., & Leithwood, K. (2007). Building and sustaining successful principalship: Key themes. In K. Leithwood & C. Day (Eds.), *Successful school leadership in times of change* (pp. 171-188). Toronto, Canada: Springer.

Day, C., Sammons, P., Hopkins, D., Harris, A., Leithwood, K., Gu, Q., et al. (2009). *The impact of school leadership on pupil outcomes.* Research report DCSF-RR108. London, UK: Department for Children, Schools and Families.

Day, C., Sammons, P., Hopkins, D., Harris, A., Leithwood, K., Gu, Q., et al. (2010). *10 strong claims about successful school leadership.* Nottingham, UK: National College for Leadership of Schools and Children's Services.

Donaldson, G. A. (2008). *How leaders learn: Cultivating capacities for school improvement.* New York, NY: Teachers College Press.

Donaldson, G. A., Bowe, L. M., McKenzie, S. V., & Marnik, G. F. (2004). Learning from leadership work: Maine pioneers a school leadership network. *Phi Delta Kappan, 85*(7), 539–544.

Duignan, P., & Gurr, D. (Eds). (2007). *Leading Australia's schools.* Winmalee, NSW: Australian Council for Educational Leaders.

Gardner, H. (1983). *Frames of mind: The theory of multiple intelligences.* New York, NY: Basic Books.

Giles, C. (2007). Building capacity in US schools: An exploration of successful leadership practice in relation to organizational learning. *International Studies in Educational Administration, 35*(3), 30–38.

Goleman, D., Boyatzis, R., & McKee, A. (2002). *The new leaders: Transforming the art of leadership into the science of results.* New York, NY: Timewarner.

Goodlad, J. I. (2006). *What schools are for: Stimulating necessary dialogue for the reconstruction of schools in our democracy.* Bloomington, IN: Phi Delta Kappan International.

Hargreaves, A. (2011). Fusion and the future of leadership. In J. Robertson & H. Timperley (Eds.), *Leadership and learning* (pp. 227–242). London, UK: Sage Publications.

Harris, A. (2005). Distributed leadership. In B. Davies (Ed.), *The essentials of school leadership* (pp. 160–172). London, UK: Paul Chapman & Corwin Press.

Harris, A. (2008). *Distributed school leadership: Developing tomorrow's leaders*. Abingdon, UK: Routledge.

Harris, A., & Muijs, D. (2005). *Improving schools through teacher leadership*. Maidenhead, UK: Open University Press.

Hoog, J., & Johansson, O. (2005). Successful principalship: The Swedish case. *Journal of Educational Administration*, 43(6), 595–606.

Jirasinghe, D., & Lyons, G. (1996). *The competent head: A job analysis of heads' tasks and personality factors*. London, UK: Falmer Press.

Johnson, L. (2007). Rethinking successful school leadership in challenging US schools: Culturally responsive practices in school–community relationships. *International Studies in Educational Administration*, 35(3), 49–57.

Kouzes, J. M., & Posner, B. Z. (2007). *The leadership challenge* (4th ed.). San Francisco, CA: John Wiley & Sons.

Leithwood, K., Harris, A., & Strauss, T. (2010). *Leading school turnaround: How successful leaders transform low-performing schools*. San Francisco, CA: Jossey-Bass.

Leithwood, K., Jacobson, S. L., & Ylimaki, R. M. (2011). Converging policy trends. In R. M. Ylimaki & S. L. Jacobson (Eds.), *US and cross-national policies, practices and preparation* (pp. 17–28). Dordrecht, The Netherlands: Springer.

Milstein, M. M., & Henry, D. A. (2008). *Leadership for resilient schools and communities*. Thousand Oaks, CA: Corwin Press.

Ministry of Education. (1996). *Te whāriki: He whāriki mātauranga mō ngā mokopuna o Aotearoa: Early childhood curriculum*. Wellington: Learning Media.

Ministry of Education. (2007). *The New Zealand curriculum*. Wellington: Learning Media.

Notman, R. (2008). Leading from within: A values-based model of principal self-development. *Leading and Managing*, 14(1), 1–15.

Notman, R. (2009). In pursuit of excellence: A leadership story. *Journal of Educational Leadership, Policy and Practice*, 24(1), 26–31.

Notman, R. (in press). A values-led principalship: The person within the professional. In C. Day & D. Gurr (Eds.), *Successful leadership in times of challenge: International perspectives*. Routledge.

Notman R., & Henry, D. A. (2009). The human face of principalship: A synthesis of case study findings. *Journal of Educational Leadership, Policy and Practice*, 24(1), 37–52.

Notman, R., & Henry, D. A. (in press). Building and sustaining successful school leadership in New Zealand. *Journal of Leadership and Policy in Schools*, 10, 1-20.

Robinson, V., Hohepa, M., & Lloyd, C. (2009). *School leadership and student outcomes: Identifying what works and why. Best evidence synthesis iteration*. Wellington: Ministry of Education.

Southworth, G. (2002). What is important in educational administration: Learning-centred school leadership. *New Zealand Journal of Educational Leadership*, 17, 5-19.

Spillane, J., Healey, K., Parise, L. M., & Kenney, A. (2011). A distributed perspective on learning leadership. In J. Robertson & H. Timperley (Eds.). *Leadership and learning* (pp. 159–171). London, UK: Sage Publications.

Stoll, L. (2010, September). *Stimulating learning conversations*. Keynote address at the Australian Council for Educational Leadership Conference, Sydney, Australia.

Timperley, H. (2009). Distributing leadership to improve outcomes for students. In K. Leithwood, B. Mascall, & T. Strauss (Eds.), *Distributed leadership according to the evidence* (pp. 197–222). New York, NY: Routledge.

Vedoy, G., & Moller, J. (2007). Successful school leadership for diversity? Examining two contrasting examples of working for democracy in Norway. *International Studies in Educational Administration*, 35(3), 58–66.

West-Burnham, J. (1997). Reflections on leadership in self-managing schools. In B. Davies & L. Ellison (Eds.), *School leadership for the 21st century* (pp. 135–143). London, UK: Routledge.

Woods, P. (2005). *Democratic leadership in education.* London, UK: Paul Chapman.

Ylimaki, R. M. (2007). Instructional leadership in challenging US schools. *International Studies in Educational Administration*, 35(3), 11–19.

Editor and contributors

Editor

Ross Notman is director of the Centre for Educational Leadership and Administration at the University of Otago. He was foundation head of department, Education Studies and Professional Practice, at the new University of Otago College of Education, and visiting fellow to the Teacher and Leadership Research Centre at the University of Nottingham in 2009. He was awarded the Minolta Dame Jean Herbison Scholarship in 2005, and a Fulbright Travel Scholarship in 2010.

He is the New Zealand project director of an international study, across 14 countries, into the leadership practices of successful school principals, and the director of a New Zealand government-funded research project (the Teaching and Learning Research Initiative, or TLRI) that examines values teaching and learning in the New Zealand school curriculum. Ross presents at international leadership conferences and has edited a significant journal publication about successful leaders in New Zealand schools.

Contributors

Alaster Gibson is a lecturer in the primary teacher education programme at Bethlehem Tertiary Institute, Tauranga. His PhD research inquired into the meaning of "Spirituality in principal leadership and its influence on teachers and teaching." For the past 7 years Alaster has led a Diploma in Teaching Studies programme in the Kingdom of Tonga. His research interests are in teacher leadership within special character school contexts.

Annie Henry is a partner in the Resiliency Group and a retired professor and department chair of educational leadership at New Mexico Highlands University. She is the immediate past president of the New Zealand Educational Administration and Leadership Society. Her research interests focus on developing school organisations through effective leadership, resilience change and organisation development. She has worked with programmes that build resilient youth and adults in New Zealand and internationally.

Jeremy Kedian is a senior lecturer in the Department of Professional Studies in Education at the University of Waikato's Faculty of Education, and is the manager and senior consultant for the University's Educational Leadership Centre. He works in a number of countries each year. Core research focuses are effective and successful leadership, non-technicist perspectives of becoming effective, and exploration of the heuristic process by which educational leaders become expert.

Darrell Latham is the manager, Professional Education Services, at the University of Otago College of Education and a staff member of the Centre for Educational Leadership and Administration. He has been an integral member of the International Successful School Principalship Project since 2008, with a focus on the sustained success of primary principals. Darrell is a regular contributor to policy debate on education and leadership issues in the New Zealand press.

Susan Lovett is a principal lecturer at the University of Canterbury in the School of Educational Studies and Human Development, where she teaches postgraduate courses in educational leadership. Susan's teaching and research interests relate to leadership learning throughout all career stages, coaching and mentoring colleagues, and school and community partnerships related to curriculum developments.

Paul Potaka is the principal of Nelson Central School. He was a researcher in the New Zealand phase of the International Successful School Principalship Project and has been a contributor to the *Journal of Educational Leadership, Policy and Practice*. His research interests include educational leadership, curriculum design and implementation, and human rights in education.

Richard Smith is a senior lecturer at Monash University, Melbourne, and has taught in universities and higher education institutions in Singapore and Aotearoa New Zealand. Richard conducts research on educational leadership, educational policy, adult education and the sociology of higher education and academic identities. He has published a co-authored book and articles in national and international journals. He is a fellow of the New Zealand Educational Administration and Leadership Society and sits on the editorial board of several journals.

Kate Thornton is a lecturer in the School of Education Policy and Implementation at Victoria University of Wellington. Her research interests include educational leadership and leadership development. Kate has worked in professional development and teaching in the tertiary sector for over 10 years and has published articles on leadership in the New Zealand early childhood education sector. Kate is the national president of the New Zealand Educational and Administration Society.

Lynn Tozer is a senior lecturer in mathematics and English at the University of Otago College of Education. She has been a national and regional coordinator in the Numeracy Project and has led teacher professional development in mathematics in primary schools for 9 years. She worked closely with the Central Region Special Schools' Cluster in their development of mathematics exemplars for teachers of children with diverse learning needs.

Hine Waitere is of Ngāti Tūwharetoa, Kahungunu and Tainui descent. She is director of the Indigenous Leadership Centre at Te Whare Wānanga o Awanuiārangi. In partnership with Waikato University, Hine is director of a Ministry of Education contract to support the development of culturally responsive leadership in secondary schools. She has research interests in educational leadership, feminist issues and indigenous education.

www.ingramcontent.com/pod-product-compliance
Lightning Source LLC
Chambersburg PA
CBHW081332230426
43667CB00018B/2903